DEBT FREE!

DEBT FREE!

Your Guide to Personal Bankruptcy Without Shame

JAMES P. CAHER

· · · · · · · · · AND · · · · · · · · ·

JOHN M. CAHER

An Owl Book

HENRY HOLT AND COMPANY · NEW YORK

Henry Holt and Company, LLC
Publishers since 1866
115 West 18th Street
New York, New York 10011

Henry Holt® is a registered trademark
of Henry Holt and Company, LLC.

Library of Congress Cataloging-in-Publication Data
Caher, James P.
Debt free!: your guide to personal bankruptcy without shame/
[James P. Caher, John M. Caher].
p.   cm.
Includes index.
ISBN 0-8050-4276-8
1. Bankruptcy—United States—Popular works.
2. Debtor and creditor—United States—Popular works.
I. Caher, John M.   II. Title.
KF1524.6.C34   1996   346.73´078—dc20   95-49255
[347.30678]   CIP

First Edition 1996

Designed by Victoria Hartman

Printed in the United States of America

11   13   15   14   12   10

To the memory of our parents,
Big Jim and Fitz,
in recognition of the lessons
they taught and the
examples they set

Contents

. . . .

Acknowledgments

. . . .

A number of friends and colleagues offered specific, tangible contributions that immeasurably improved this book.

Our agent, Sheree Bykofsky of Sheree Bykofsky Associates in New York City, and her assistant, Janet Rosen, provided invaluable advice and support through the early stages. Sheree and Janet believed in us and our project and worked with us—patiently—to ensure that this book would be published. They steered us to our publisher, Henry Holt and Company, an insightful editor, David Sobel, and a patient editorial assistant and eagle-eyed production editor, Jonathan S. Landreth and Carrie A. Smith, respectively, who skillfully massaged our manuscript and egos.

Janet Mendel-Hartvig, M.D., Ph.D., and William Donnelly, Ed.D., granted us the benefit of their foresight, wisdom, and experience by carefully reading, and constructively criticizing, earlier drafts. Dr. Mendel-Hartvig and Professor Donnelly pointed out the rough spots, the typos, and the parts that were just plain unclear—and generously offered their suggestions on improving our work.

In addition, several of our friends and relatives graciously offered their support, encouragement, and love: Barbara Bower, Bunny Burnes, Erin Caher and Kerry Caher, Ray Fanning, Heather Harpham, Kirsten Hokanson, Mike McCarthy and Maureen McCarthy.

Finally, and most important, we acknowledge the love, respect, commitment—and occasionally tolerance, patience, and domestic fortitude—that could only have been provided by our respective mates, Kate Donnelly and Kathleen Caher.

To each of our supporters, we express our sincere gratitude.

Introduction

· ·

OKAY, YOU BLEW IT

Things got out of hand, and you're up to your ears in debt. Finance companies say that if you don't pay up, and soon, they are going to take your home and car. Credit card firms are threatening to sue. Debt collectors are bugging you daily.

There is a way—a perfectly legitimate, legal, honorable way—to stop foreclosures and repossessions, to put an end to lawsuits, to protect your paycheck from garnishments, and to get those pesky debt collectors off your back. The federal bankruptcy laws are designed just for people like you, offering a "fresh start" and an opportunity to get back on your feet and begin your financial life anew.

Yet the people in the credit industry don't particularly want you to know about bankruptcy, and they will deploy a number of weapons in their arsenal—guilt, shame, threat of financial blacklisting—to keep you under their thumb rather than shielded by the court. They whine and whimper about bankruptcy losses, complain endlessly to their representatives in Congress, and go to great efforts to discourage you from taking what may be the only reasonable avenue to relief: bankruptcy.

Consider these recent maneuvers:

• Visa USA, the nation's largest credit card company, initiated a program to encourage banks to challenge bankruptcy petitions in court.

• The American Bankers Association, a trade group, began a campaign to discourage people from filing bankruptcy, claiming that seeking court protection would cripple a person's credit rating for eternity and jeopardize his or her job prospects.

- Big profits from exorbitant interest rates have encouraged credit card companies to find loopholes in federal regulations against mailing unsolicited credit cards.
- Credit card companies extend credit to students with no income because, if necessary, many parents can be shamed into paying.
- A bankruptcy court in Florida recently awarded a credit card company "the greedy lender award" of the year, saying: "What kind of underwriting procedures were used by First Card Services, Inc., in approving an $8,000 cash advance to a consumer with over $40,000 in credit card debt and no income for over a year? Where did the Debtor, a 57-year-old Cuban refugee with a third grade education get this magic card in the first place? He testified that he never applied for the card. 'They sent it to him in the mail.' Is this a great country or what?"*

The credit industry, for obvious reasons, is concerned about the increase in consumer bankruptcies. But the simple fact of the matter is that *the jump in bankruptcy filings is in direct proportion to relaxed credit standards.* The credit industry has made an economic decision that more is gained by the reckless extension of credit than is lost through default. You should base your bankruptcy decision on a similar standard: Do the benefits outweigh the drawbacks?

This book will help you answer that question. It explains, in layperson's terms, the ins and outs of bankruptcy, the risks and rewards. It recognizes and sympathizes with your emotional state but encourages you to make the decision for rational reasons and to reject the threats, shame, and guilt trips laid on you by the credit industry.

HOW THIS BOOK IS ORGANIZED

Debt Free! is designed to provide you with a working knowledge of bankruptcy, as painlessly as possible.

Chapter 1 explains the hows, whys, and whats of bankruptcy.

Chapter 2 answers the most commonly asked questions about bankruptcy.

---

*In re Cruz, 179 BR 975, 978 (Bankr, S.D.Fla.1995).

Chapter 12 contains a checklist of things to remember.

Chapter 13 provides some viable—and not viable—alternatives to bankruptcy.

The meaty, technical information is in the remaining chapters. Appendix 1 describes your rights under the Fair Debt Collection Practices Act, which gives you an important shield against aggressive collectors. Appendix 2 provides various tables, outlining your options and the consequences. Appendix 3 explains how the states tailor bankruptcy laws, even though bankruptcy is mainly the prerogative of the Congress and the federal courts. Appendix 4 provides a fill-in-the-blank form to help you get a handle on your finances by developing a monthly budget. Appendix 5 is a worksheet that allows you to estimate the amount you would have to pay to creditors under a court-supervised payment plan.

Anecdotal stories in virtually every chapter put a human face on the sometimes arcane doctrines of bankruptcy law.

There are many ways to approach this book:

• If you want to learn all you can about bankruptcy, start at the beginning and read to the end.

• If you're looking for a quick overview, scan the questions and answers in chapter 2 and take a look at the anecdotes that start and end chapters 3–11 and 13 and appendix 1.

• And if you fall somewhere in between, read chapter 1, glance at the questions and answers in chapter 2, and then turn to the technical stuff, as needed. If you get bogged down with an unfamiliar term, check out the glossary.

TWO IMPORTANT NOTES

First, a new Bankruptcy Reform Act, which changed many provisions of the U.S. Bankruptcy Code, went into effect on October 22, 1994, and applies to all bankruptcies filed on or after that date. *Debt Free!* covers the changes made by the new law, but remember: if your bankruptcy was filed before October 22, 1994, the changes don't apply to your case.

Second, this book is designed as an aid to your bankruptcy. It does not pretend to be a substitute for competent legal representation.

DEBT FREE!

1

. . . .

DEBT FREE AND
SHAME FREE

When we were kids, a close friend of our father's made some unfortunate financial decisions and was forced to declare bankruptcy. We'll never forget the sight of this man, who had been a proud and successful scholar, athlete, and businessman, sitting on an empty beer case after pawning all of his furniture, weeping like a child over the humiliation and shame he brought to himself and his family. He was the neighborhood pariah, a shunned man. Surely, there was nobody else we knew who had been forced to bankruptcy court, or so we thought.

Today, bankruptcy is recognized as a perfectly respectable solution to financial distress, a legal avenue followed by all kinds of people, ranging from tycoons like the Hunt brothers to nationally known political figures like the late former Texas governor John B. Connally, to the secretary who overextended his credit cards and the executive who lived beyond her means.

In just the last eight years, filings have doubled. According to the National Coalition for Consumer Credit Rights, someone files for bankruptcy once every nine seconds. Statistics indicate that one out of twelve Americans is overwhelmed with debt. The number of filings is now more than double the level recorded in any year prior to 1986. And for every person filing bankruptcy, there are several others who should file but are deterred only by the propaganda of the credit industry.

Who are these people?

• Seventy percent of the folks seeking help from the National Coalition for Consumer Credit Rights are white-collar.

1

• Almost 60 percent of bankruptcy filers are baby boomers; the median age of filers is now thirty-seven, about ten years older than people filing in the 1960s.

• Bankruptcy filers are more likely than the national population to have graduated from high school and twice as likely to have completed some college.

• People filing bankruptcy are, overwhelmingly, homeowners.

• Many are single women, frequently those who were recently divorced.

In essence, the image of the sleazy, deadbeat bankruptcy filer is a phantom. A more accurate portrait is an ordinary, honest, hardworking, educated middle-class consumer who fell for the aggressive and sophisticated credit marketing techniques, lost control, and unwittingly surrendered his or her financial soul to the devil that is debt.

However, while bankruptcy no longer carries the scarlet letter of the past, it remains a heart-wrenching option for people who, through their own poor judgment or, more often, circumstances beyond their control, cannot make ends meet.

Sometimes people get into trouble because of ill-advised investments, failed get-rich-quick schemes, or outright foolhardiness.

As never before, educated, middle-class Americans are falling victim to a terrible con job and sinking under a consumer debt load that frequently exceeds a whole year's net income. Credit card companies are furiously pumping out cards; there are enough currently in circulation for every man, woman, and child in the country to carry four of them. Americans are living in a virtual house of (credit) cards that will topple with the slightest wind, the smallest income disruption.

Creditors are more than willing to ignore the dangers of tomorrow so they can reap exorbitant interest rates today. They are counting on—literally banking on—your ignorance. They encourage robbing Peter to pay Paul by using credit card advances to pay off credit card bills. They have convinced many middle-class consumers to bleed all the equity out of their homes through aggressively marketed home equity loans.

The early experience with our father's friend taught us that most debtors are not necessarily reckless spendthrifts or deadbeats. Rather, they are people who, without the help of the court, would remain caught in a downward spiral of debt.

Whatever the cause for a person's financial difficulty, the U.S.

Bankruptcy Code was enacted to help the honest debtor start over. With the aid of the bankruptcy court, our father's friend was able to climb out of a financial abyss, resurrect his career, raise a family in a nice home, and eventually retire comfortably.

And so can you.

The key is to recognize the subtle, and not so subtle, pressures of the credit industry and, most important, to acknowledge that the ultimate responsibility is yours. Bankruptcy can be a viable and rational first step to regaining control. The courts and the law will show you the way and your lawyer should be a comforting guide, but you have to begin blazing this trail by yourself.

THE "FRESH START" PRINCIPLE

Bankruptcy has been around since there has been money and ways to lose it. What's changed over the centuries is the way society deals with the people who can't pay their bills.

For eons, debtors were tossed in prison to be punished for their financial miscues. The Enlightenment thinkers who formed the government in this country, however, realized that jailing honest debtors was unfair and kind of stupid. They set the stage for today's bankruptcy relief by giving Congress the muscle to enact uniform laws. Congress took the hint and adopted various bankruptcy statutes, most recently the Bankruptcy Reform Act of 1994.

The key feature of American bankruptcy is the "fresh start" principle, which recognizes that society as a whole benefits when debt-ridden people are given a chance for financial rebirth, permitting them to get back on their feet and start building financially secure lives for themselves and their families. Bankruptcy laws are designed to give you an opportunity to begin your financial life anew.

The concept was eloquently articulated by Justice William R. Day in the *Wetmore v. Markoe** decision of 1904: "Systems of bankruptcy are designed to relieve the honest debtor from the weight of indebtedness which has become oppressive and to permit him to have a fresh start in . . . life, freed from the obligation and responsibilities which may have resulted from . . . misfortunes."

If you qualify, federal law will allow you to reorganize your fi-

---

* 25 S.Ct. 172, 176 (1904)

nances and gradually pay off your obligations under the protection of the court—without having to sacrifice your belongings.

BANKRUPTCY IS NOT ABOUT GUILT

Much more recently, the U.S. Supreme Court noted in the 1991 case of *Grogan v. Garner** that ". . . a central purpose of the Code is to provide a procedure by which certain insolvent debtors can re-order their affairs, make peace with their creditors, and enjoy a new opportunity in life with a clear field for future effort, unhampered by the pressure and discouragement of pre-existing debt."

Very few debtors, viewing their financial instability as a sign of character weakness and fearing social stigma, go through bankruptcy without paying a stiff emotional price. They toil for years, making partial payments, but because of exorbitant interest rates, never even make a dent in their bills. Often, people struggle, painfully and needlessly, to avoid bankruptcy, reasoning that their credit history will be better this way. The cruel truth is just the opposite: a person is actually a better credit risk after bankruptcy because he or she has no other debts and can't file bankruptcy for another six years.

Aside from getting a lawyer to sue you, the two most powerful weapons of bill collectors are the use of guilt, sort of a psychological warfare technique, and the threat that bankruptcy will destroy your ability to get future credit.

Don't let them snow you.

When the bank lent you money or the credit card company sent you a "preapproved" card inviting you to "live your dreams today," they knew full well that someday you might have to take advantage of the relief Congress provided under the Bankruptcy Code. In fact, they planned on it.

Lending institutions try to predict what portion of their accounts will end in bankruptcy. If there are fewer bankruptcies than predicted, they conclude that their credit policies are too strict, and become even more aggressive in trying to attract new borrowers. Even though bankruptcies have risen sharply over the years, the competition among credit card companies remains fierce, with new companies entering the market all the time.

---

* 111 S.Ct. 654, 659 (1991)

Consider the following facts and conclusions from national surveys:

• Despite their incessant complaining, creditors spend more for postage stamps to bill current customers and lure new ones than they do to cover their losses.

• Creditors are at least partially to blame for any losses because of irresponsible lending practices.

• Although the credit industry would have you believe that people recklessly and shamelessly turn to bankruptcy so they can stiff their creditors, the facts show that people are far more inclined to make every effort—even unreasonable efforts—to avoid bankruptcy.

• Two bellwether studies of bankruptcy filers—by researchers Teresa A. Sullivan and Jay Lawrence Westbrook of the University of Texas at Austin and Elizabeth Warren of the University of Pennsylvania—came to the same, clear conclusion: with few exceptions, the people who file for bankruptcy are drowning in debt; cases of abuse are rare and atypical; credit card companies are increasingly reaching out to low-income consumers.

• Some major credit card companies are now using computer programs to predict not only how many customers will file for bankruptcy but which ones. Yet they still extend credit to those people, despite the risk.

Regardless, you—the debtor—are ultimately responsible. While the credit industry vultures may have preyed on your weaknesses or exploited your ignorance, you got yourself into this mess. And only you can get yourself out.

HANDLING BILL COLLECTORS

Under the federal Fair Debt Collection Practices Act (see appendix 1), debt collectors cannot communicate with other persons concerning your debt, may not call you before 8 A.M. or after 9 P.M. or at any other time they know to be inconvenient, and can't bug you at work without your employer's permission. Moreover, if you tell a debt collector, in writing, to leave you alone, that individual may not be allowed to contact you further. In any case, a debt collector can't threaten you with force or use foul or abusive language.

Sandy was doing her best to pay her bills but had fallen severely behind. Bill collectors were hounding her, calling at all hours, and threatening to squeal to her employer. She told them to take a hike, and—by law—they had to. Because she knew federal law prohibits such bullying and even imposes fines on overzealous collectors, Sandy was able to turn the tables on the bill collectors and scare them off.

Some debt collectors are stereotypical bullies. If you let them intimidate you, they will. If you tell them to buzz off, they'd better, or they may face legal sanctions themselves.

Neither the courts nor juries are willing to tolerate such bullies. A case in point is a 1995 jury verdict in El Paso, Texas. A couple with a $2,000 credit card debt was subjected to harassing, profanity-laced telephone calls from collection agents. Jurors found that the credit company violated the Texas Debt Collection Practices Act, and awarded the couple $11 million in compensatory and punitive damages.

DO YOU NEED A LAWYER?

Yes. But how are you going to pay for a lawyer if you don't have any money? Don't worry about it now. In chapter 2, "Questions and Answers," we will give you some pointers on raising the money to file bankruptcy. Also, in some cases, part of the attorney fees can be covered by the bankruptcy plan. In any event, don't let the fear of legal expenses keep you from hiring a lawyer.

In the last few years, partially in response to the relatively high fees of attorneys, a number of paralegals and "document" preparation services have offered do-it-yourself bankruptcy programs. Good idea? Put it this way: You could try to cross the highway with your eyes closed, and you might make it. But do you really want to try?

Sure, you can buy the fill-in-the-blank forms and do it yourself. But if you goof or overlook something or the form doesn't reflect some obscure change in the law, you may permanently jeopardize your rights. And then what are you going to do, sue yourself for malpractice?

Bankruptcy appears simple only to those who don't know any better. While the Bankruptcy Code is only a single volume, since 1978 the courts have produced 185 volumes of decisions interpreting the law, and this continues at the rate of about 12 volumes a year.

Not only is it a mistake to try to handle your own bankruptcy, it's also probably a mistake to seek advice from anyone other than a bankruptcy specialist. You may want to think twice about hiring your cousin Oscar, the divorce attorney who occasionally dabbles in bankruptcy. Despite his best efforts and intentions, he may inadvertently make a mistake that seriously compromises your rights.

Why, then, should you take the time to learn about bankruptcy when you may end up paying a lawyer anyway? There are several reasons:

• The information in *Debt Free!* will enable you to judge whether the lawyer you are considering knows what he or she is doing. Unfortunately, some lawyers still try to practice bankruptcy law on a part-time basis, and they can't possibly keep up on everything they need to know.

• Many bankruptcy lawyers, in order to reduce fees, rely heavily on paralegals or other nonlawyers. Some of these folks are wonderfully competent; others are bumbling buffoons. If they screw up, it's you who will pay.

Debt Free! will help you make a wise choice in lawyers and serve as a safety net to clear up any miscommunication between you and the lawyer. If the lawyer or paralegal tells you something that doesn't jibe with what's in this book, check it out.

It might be that, because of some peculiar feature of local law, the lawyer is right. On the other hand, by bringing the discrepancy to the lawyer's attention, you might clear up a misunderstanding that has developed without your realizing it.

Make no mistake about it: filing bankruptcy is a serious matter and can have serious consequences. This book is a supplement, not a replacement, for professional advice. There's an old saying that a lawyer who represents himself has a fool for a client. Nowhere is this more true than in bankruptcy.

GETTING YOUR LIFE BACK IN ORDER

Bankruptcy is never an easy decision to make, nor is it an easy process to endure. However, in many, many instances it is a financial lifeline that grants you a chance to put your financial life back together.

Just as our father's friend took hold of his problems and put the difficult years behind him, so can you. The Bankruptcy Code was created to help people like him, and perhaps people like you.

2

QUESTIONS AND ANSWERS

WHAT TYPES OF BANKRUPTCY PROTECTION ARE AVAILABLE?

Depending on your individual situation, you are probably eligible for either a *Chapter 7* bankruptcy, in which your debts are wiped out and some of your assets may be transferred to a court-appointed trustee; or a *Chapter 13* bankruptcy, in which you hang on to all your assets and have an opportunity to establish a workable repayment plan.

In sum, Chapter 7 discharges all your debts, in return for the surrender of what is called *nonexempt property of the estate;* Chapter 13 involves a repayment plan where you pay all or a part of your debts over a period of thirty-six to sixty months.

For more information, see the section on types of bankruptcy in chapter 3, "A Bird's-Eye View."

WILL I LOSE MY HOME?

Probably not.

But that depends on whether you are behind in mortgage payments, how much your house is worth, and the state in which you live. When all is said and done, few people lose their home solely because they filed bankruptcy.

See chapter 9, "Home Sweet Home."

WILL I LOSE MY CAR?

Probably not.

If the car is financed, you will have to continue making payments if you want to keep the vehicle. In a Chapter 13 case it may be possible to reduce the payments to a more affordable amount. If you don't want to keep the car, you can simply give it back without further obligation.

After Dan filed bankruptcy, the finance company took his car and refused to give it back. Not only did the court make the company return the car, it fined the firm $3,000. Reason: Once a bankruptcy petition is filed, an *automatic stay* goes into effect. It stops creditors from garnishing wages, repossessing property, or even contacting debtors.

See the section on automobiles in chapter 8, "Cars and Household Goods."

WILL I LOSE MY PERSONAL BELONGINGS?

Probably not.

In the vast majority of consumer bankruptcy cases, debtors retain all of their personal and household belongings.

See chapter 5, "What Do You Have to Lose?"

CAN FILING BANKRUPTCY
SAVE ME FROM AN EVICTION?

Quite possibly.

You can stop the eviction if you file Chapter 13 before your leasehold interest is actually terminated under the provisions of local law. You can pay past-due rent under the plan and pay current rent as you go along.

But take note: this is a legitimate strategy only if you truly intend to pay the back rent. In some parts of the country, unscrupulous bankruptcy mills have encouraged people to file a Chapter 13 to stop an eviction, allow the case to be dismissed, and then file a new Chapter 13 each time the landlord tries to evict. Courts are fed up with this ploy and have been fining people who try it.

WILL BANKRUPTCY AFFECT MY CREDIT RATING?

Yes.

A bankruptcy filing will remain on your credit report for ten years, but you can take steps right now to lay the groundwork for repairing your credit. See "Groundwork for Credit Repair" in chapter 3, "A Bird's-Eye View."

Don't pay too much attention to the horror stories bill collectors tell you about the effect of bankruptcy on your credit. If you talk to people who have actually filed bankruptcy, you'll discover that with a little work and perseverance, you can reestablish credit soon after bankruptcy. See "Credit Repair" in chapter 10, "Life After Bankruptcy."

WILL BANKRUPTCY AFFECT MY JOB?

No.

Employment discrimination is illegal. Federal law prohibits employers from firing or in any way discriminating against you because of a bankruptcy petition.

If your wages are being garnished, your employer might actually prefer that you file bankruptcy, so he or she doesn't have to deal with the paperwork anymore.

See "Nondiscrimination Laws" in chapter 10, "Life After Bankruptcy."

MY MOM COSIGNED ONE OF MY DEBTS.
WHAT WILL HAPPEN TO HER IF I FILE BANKRUPTCY?

It depends. If you file a Chapter 7, your mom is completely vulnerable and will not be protected at all. Even though your obligation is discharged, the creditor could come after your mother immediately. So what is in your best interests may be contrary to your mother's.

But if you file a Chapter 13, your mom would be shielded from creditors, assuming your plan provided for payment of that debt in full over the life of the Chapter 13.

See the discussion of cosigned debts in chapter 3, "A Bird's-Eye View."

SHOULD I FILE BANKRUPTCY BEFORE I GET MARRIED?

Probably.

If one spouse files bankruptcy, the other spouse does not have to file and the credit of the nonfiling spouse theoretically should not be affected. But this doesn't mean that credit-reporting bureaus will report it correctly, so you may have to straighten things out later.

It's easier if you file before you get married. That way, your spouse's name will not be associated with your bankruptcy in any way.

I'M MARRIED. DOES MY SPOUSE HAVE TO FILE BANKRUPTCY IF I DO?

No.

Many married people think that they are automatically responsible for each other's debts. Not so. In most cases your spouse is not responsible for your debts unless he or she expressly agreed to pay.

If most of the debts are in your name exclusively, your spouse doesn't have to file bankruptcy. But if many of your debts are joint obligations, both you and your spouse probably need to file. If only you file, joint creditors can still go after your spouse, unless you file Chapter 13 and propose to pay the joint debts in full. Confusing, isn't it? See the section on cosigned debts in chapter 3, "A Bird's-Eye View."

Even in situations where you and your spouse must both file bankruptcy, you don't have to file jointly. And sometimes it's best not to. See the section on jointly held property in chapter 9, "Home Sweet Home."

HOW WILL BANKRUPTCY AFFECT MY SPOUSE?

If you and your spouse don't owe any joint debts, or don't own property together, your spouse shouldn't be affected. But the court-appointed trustee will question you to make sure that you haven't transferred assets to your spouse or deposited money in his or her bank account to protect it from creditors. See the section on friends and lovers in chapter 7, "Games People Play."

MY BOYFRIEND AND I LIVE TOGETHER, AND MOST OF OUR DEBTS ARE JOINT. CAN WE FILE A JOINT BANKRUPTCY?

No.

You must actually be married to file a joint bankruptcy. If you each file separately, the court might consolidate your cases, but this wouldn't save you from having to pay two court filing fees.

MY GIRLFRIEND AND I MAINTAIN A JOINT BANK ACCOUNT. CAN THE TRUSTEE GET MY GIRLFRIEND'S MONEY?

In theory, no.

You will, however, have to be able to show what portion of the account represents your girlfriend's money. See the section on friends and lovers in chapter 7, "Games People Play."

WHAT IF I AM ALREADY BEING SUED?

Filing a bankruptcy petition stops any lawsuits in progress and prevents any new ones from being started. In addition, any wage garnishments will be stopped immediately. This is because of the *automatic stay*, a court order that goes into effect the minute your bankruptcy petition is filed with the court. The automatic stay forbids creditors from taking further action against you or your property without first getting the court's permission. See the "Automatic Stay" section in chapter 3, "A Bird's-Eye View."

But if you own your home, it may be important to file bankruptcy before a judgment is actually entered against you in a lawsuit. See the discussion of judgment liens in chapter 9, "Home Sweet Home."

WILL FILING BANKRUPTCY WIPE OUT UNPAID INCOME TAX BILLS?

In most cases, no.

However, in a Chapter 13 case you can pay off your taxes over three to five years, frequently without interest or penalties. See the section on income taxes in chapter 4, "Forgive Us Our Trespasses."

WILL BANKRUPTCY AFFECT MY ABILITY TO GET STUDENT LOANS IN THE FUTURE?

It shouldn't.

The 1994 amendments forbid discrimination against a student loan applicant based on bankruptcy. See the nondiscrimination portions of chapter 10, "Life After Bankruptcy."

CAN MY COLLEGE REFUSE TO ISSUE TRANSCRIPTS IF I FILE BANKRUPTCY?

Maybe. The courts have reached different conclusions on this issue.

Timing might be critical. If you think you'll need transcripts in the near future, tell your lawyer before filing bankruptcy. Most courts insist that schools issue transcripts if you request them within a few months after filing bankruptcy. However, you may still have to pay a small "administrative fee" to get them.

HOW LONG DOES IT TAKE TO FILE BANKRUPTCY?

Your petition can be filed within a matter of days. Once the petition is on file, you are on your way to a fresh start in life. The petition gets creditors off your back, stops lawsuits, foreclosures, and other collection activities.

About forty days after your petition is filed, you and your attorney will attend a meeting of creditors (called a *341 meeting*). Within four months of the petition date, most Chapter 7 cases are finished and closed. Chapter 13 cases remain open for the life of the repayment plan, which runs from three to five years.

WILL I HAVE TO GO TO COURT?

Probably not.

In the vast majority of consumer bankruptcy cases, the debtor never has to appear in court.

WHAT WILL IT COST TO FILE A BANKRUPTCY PETITION?

The court filing fee is $175 for Chapter 7 and $160 for Chapter 13.

Legal fees vary, depending on where you live. In a Chapter 7 they usually range from $300 to $1,000. Fees for a Chapter 13 may be higher, but part of the fees can usually be included in the repayment plan.

I'M BROKE. WHERE DO I GET THE MONEY TO FILE BANKRUPTCY?

There are lots of steps to take, and the first is to recognize that once you make the decision to file bankruptcy, you shouldn't make any more payments on debts that will ultimately be wiped out. That alone might free up some cash. See "The Trustee's Avoidance Powers" in chapter 7, "Games People Play."

You could also sell some assets to raise the money. This is a smart move if you would otherwise lose these assets when you file bankruptcy. See chapter 5, "What Do You Have to Lose?"

Also, a friend or relative might advance the money. It's not uncommon for an employer to pay bankruptcy fees to get the employee's attention focused on the job instead of his or her financial problems, and to avoid the hassle of dealing with creditors trying to attach or garnish wages.

On the other hand, don't borrow money from anyone without revealing your plan to file bankruptcy, or you might get socked for fraud. See chapter 4, "Forgive Us Our Trespasses," particularly the section on debts arising from fraud or other misconduct.

MUST I BE AN AMERICAN CITIZEN TO BE ELIGIBLE FOR BANKRUPTCY?

No.

Neither citizenship, nor even formal resident-alien status, is required. Bankruptcy is available if you live in the United States or have a business or property here.

DO I HAVE TO BE EMPLOYED TO QUALIFY FOR A CHAPTER 13 PAYMENT PROGRAM?

No.

You do need a source of income, however. It can be alimony, welfare, odd jobs, contributions from family members, or any other source that is stable and regular enough to cover the payments required by your Chapter 13 plan.

The 1994 amendments also make Chapter 13 a viable way to reorganize a business if you are self-employed. But Chapter 13 is still not available to corporations or partnerships.

See the discussion of Chapter 13 eligibility in chapter 3, "A Bird's-Eye View."

IF I CHANGE MY MIND AFTER FILING,
CAN I CANCEL MY BANKRUPTCY?

It depends on whether you filed a Chapter 7 or a Chapter 13. You can dismiss a Chapter 13 but not a Chapter 7. However, even if you dismiss, your credit reports may still show a bankruptcy.

WHAT HAPPENS IF MY BANKRUPTCY IS DISMISSED?

The court mails all your creditors a notice saying that the case is dismissed, the automatic stay (which suspends debt collection activities) is no longer in effect, and they are free to resume collection efforts and foreclosures. But, as a practical matter, many creditors don't bother. They've already written the debt off, at least in their own mind.

I FILED BANKRUPTCY SEVERAL
YEARS AGO. CAN I FILE AGAIN?

Maybe.

You may not be eligible to refile for 180 days (under the *180-day rule*, which generally prohibits filing a bankruptcy petition within 180 days of a previously dismissed petition) if the case was dismissed:

- at your request after a creditor asked the court for relief from the automatic stay, or
- because you intentionally disobeyed an order of the court, such as the order to appear at the 341 meeting.

Assuming that your bankruptcy was not dismissed under these circumstances, the answer depends on whether you want to file a Chapter 7 or Chapter 13.

If you were granted a discharge in a bankruptcy case filed less than six years ago (unless it was a Chapter 13 where creditors were paid at least 70 percent of their claims), you cannot discharge your debts in a Chapter 7. You can file a Chapter 13 case, however, provided you were not trying to improperly manipulate the Bankruptcy Code with multiple filings. See chapter 11, "You Blew It Again?"

THE BANK HAS STARTED FORECLOSURE PROCEEDINGS. IS IT TOO LATE TO FILE BANKRUPTCY AND SAVE MY HOME?

No.

But note that you need to see a bankruptcy lawyer immediately. When you call for an initial appointment, be sure to inform the lawyer that foreclosure proceedings are under way.

Under the 1994 amendments you have until the foreclosure sale, and possibly longer, if you have *redemption* rights under state law. Redemption rights give you a certain amount of time to buy back the property after foreclosure.

A Chapter 13, if filed in time, will allow you to make up back mortgage payments over three to five years. See the section on keeping your residence in chapter 9, "Home Sweet Home."

MY CAR HAS BEEN REPOSSESSED. CAN I GET IT BACK?

It depends on whether you file bankruptcy in time. A creditor must go through two steps to wipe out your interest in the car: (1) actually seize (repossess) the car and (2) sell it, usually at an auction. You can get your car back if you file before the auction is held.

The amount you'll have to pay to get the car back depends on which chapter you file under.

• If you file a Chapter 7, you will have to pay off the entire loan in a lump sum within a short time, about thirty days after the petition date.

• In a Chapter 13, however, you could get the car back by proposing a plan where you pay only the value of the car and make these payments over three to five years.

See the "Automobiles" section in chapter 8, "Cars and Household Goods."

CAN I EXCLUDE SOME DEBTS FROM MY BANKRUPTCY?

No.

There is a popular misconception that people can pick and choose whom they want to list in their bankruptcy. Everyone to whom you owe money must be listed. See "Unscheduled Debts" in chapter 4, "Forgive Us Our Trespasses."

Naturally, if you don't owe a person money on the petition date, that individual is not listed. But be careful. You should not make any significant payments to creditors on the eve of bankruptcy without first talking to your lawyer. See "Preferential Transfers" in chapter 7, "Games People Play."

If you wish, you can also voluntarily repay any creditor after you file. And you can always continue regular house or car payments so these creditors are not affected by your bankruptcy.

WILL MY DOCTORS REFUSE TO TREAT ME IF I CLAIM BANKRUPTCY ON THEIR BILLS?

Most doctors have seen a lot of bankruptcies and realize that it is the only alternative for many folks. You should contact the doctors' offices either before, or shortly after, filing and explain the situation. In most cases satisfactory arrangements can be worked out.

Generally, you shouldn't make any significant payments on doctor bills just before filing. See "Preferential Transfers" in chapter 7, "Games People Play."

WHAT CAN MY CREDITORS DO IF
I DON'T FILE BANKRUPTCY?

We discuss the alternatives to bankruptcy in chapter 13, "Debt Free Without Bankruptcy." In general, if you choose to do nothing, a creditor's powers depend on how, and whether, the debt is secured:

• *Claims secured by your car.* If a debt is secured by your car, the creditor can repossess the vehicle and sell it to pay the loan. Usually, the proceeds of a repossession sale are not enough to pay the debt, so you will still be responsible for the balance. The law requires the creditor to sell the car in a "commercially reasonable" manner, but this doesn't mean that the creditor will get nearly as much as you could be selling it yourself.

• *Claims secured by your home.* If the claim is secured by your house, the creditor can foreclose. Most foreclosures take at least ninety days, and you can continue to live on the property until the foreclosure is completed. See the "No Equity" section of chapter 9, "Home Sweet Home."

• *Taxes.* The IRS has truly scary powers to seize your bank account, pension, real property, or maybe even the shirt off your back. (Dealing with the IRS is discussed in chapter 13, "Debt Free Without Bankruptcy.") State taxing authorities also have special powers, and some states allow these powers to be used to collect student loans that have been guaranteed by the state.

• *Other claims.* Creditors with other types of claims can't do much without first suing you and getting a judgment. To do this, they must serve you with legal documents and give you a chance to dispute the debt in court. If you don't respond, a default judgment can be entered against you.

WHAT IF THE CREDITOR HAS
A JUDGMENT AGAINST ME?

A creditor with a judgment can go after your property to the extent that it is not *exempt*. See chapter 5, "What Do You Have to Lose?" to find out what property is exempt.

If all your property is exempt, there is nothing more the creditor can do for the time being. But judgments last a long time—as long as twenty years in some states. So a judgment creditor can wait around hoping you will eventually acquire some nonexempt property.

Also, if you own real property that is subject to a judgment lien, you couldn't sell it without first paying the judgment. But if you file bankruptcy, you may be able to cancel judgment liens. See "Your Avoidance Powers" in chapter 7, "Games People Play."

Even if a judgment creditor can't get any of your property, that creditor can still haul you into court for a *debtors' exam.* At this exam you have to tell the creditor about any nonexempt property you have, and, theoretically, the creditor could send the sheriff out to seize the property and sell it. In practice, this doesn't usually happen unless a judgment debtor owns some unusually valuable item of property. In some states the sheriff could sell your home if you have nonexempt equity in it.

If you are served with an actual court order requiring you to appear for such an examination, don't ignore it. If you ignore a summons and complaint, the worst that can happen is that a judgment will be entered against you; if you disregard an order for a debtors' exam, you can be held in contempt of court and sent to jail.

The good news is that if you file bankruptcy before the date of the debtors' exam, you don't have to go. This is because the automatic stay goes into effect. See the discussion in chapter 3, "A Bird's-Eye View."

MY WAGES HAVE JUST BEEN GARNISHED. WILL I LOSE ALL MY PAY?

No.

Federal law limits the amount that can be garnished from your paycheck. You must be left with at least 75 percent of your net pay or thirty times the federal minimum wage, whichever is greater. In addition, many states have laws that allow you to keep even more. See the "Wages" section of chapter 5, "What Do You Have to Lose?"

But there are two important exceptions:

• *IRS garnishments.* The amount of pay protected from IRS seizure is very small. It's an amount equal to your standard deduction with personal exemptions allowable for the year, divided by fifty-two.

• *Garnishments for support.* The exemption can be as small as thirty-five percent of your net pay.

IF I DON'T OWN ANYTHING, DO I STILL NEED BANKRUPTCY?

Maybe.

Bankruptcy will stop the harassment and lawsuits, protect future wages from garnishment, and wipe the slate clean so you can start rebuilding your life. See the "Credit Repair" section in chapter 10, "Life After Bankruptcy."

If you're burdened with debts you will never realistically be able to pay, ignoring the problem won't make it go away—not in any reasonable amount of time, anyway. In short, bankruptcy may be the only way to truly turn your life around and get a fresh start.

See "Ignoring Creditors" in chapter 13, "Debt Free Without Bankruptcy."

WHAT IS THE STATUTE OF LIMITATIONS ON DEBTS?

In most cases the statute of limitations is six years. If a judgment has been entered, it can be as long as twenty years.

The trick is figuring when the clock starts to run. Sometimes, just making partial payments or acknowledging the debt can start the time running all over again.

Also, be aware that Congress canceled state statutes of limitations on student loans, in favor of the time limits contained in the Bankruptcy Code. See "Student Loans" in chapter 4, "Forgive Us Our Trespasses."

WHEN IS BANKRUPTCY NOT THE SOLUTION?

Bankruptcy is the wrong route if you are just trying to avoid wage garnishment, because only a quarter of your earnings can be used to take care of a court judgment. Moreover, it's not the way to stop an eviction unless you are serious about going through with a Chapter 13 plan.

In fact, filing bankruptcy solely to delay foreclosures or lawsuits with no intention of following through is wrong, probably won't work (not for very long anyway), and may get you fined.

Basically, it's the wrong solution if your motive is anything other than wanting relief from your debts, or if you are unwilling to fulfill your responsibilities as a debtor under the Bankruptcy Code.

3

A BIRD'S-EYE VIEW

Skinflint Homer—the kind of guy who always tries to stretch one extra shave out of his disposable safety razor and routinely walks around with little Band-Aids on his face—figured he'd cut expenses by hiring Acme Bankruptcy Service to handle his case. As usual, Homer was penny-wise and pound-foolish. He was shocked to find out, after bankruptcy, that he still owed a $6,000 student loan, that the IRS was still on his back, that his cherished fishing boat was history—and that his credit was shot. It didn't have to be that way.

Bankruptcy law fills volumes and volumes of incredibly dull books. This chapter is designed to give you a bird's-eye view of the bankruptcy process. It won't make a lawyer out of you, but it will give you a working knowledge of bankruptcy.

This chapter explains:

- important bankruptcy terms
- different types of bankruptcy
- eligibility requirements
- bankruptcy procedures
- the players and their role in the process.

IMPORTANT TERMS

The legal meanings of words are often different from their everyday usage. It's a good idea to know some legalese so you are at least talking the same language as the legal eagles you'll encounter on the route to bankruptcy. Although the glossary defines many of the terms of bankruptcy proceedings listed here, it is important to be familiar with several of them before going any further.

- **Automatic stay.** A court order that goes into effect the minute a bankruptcy petition is filed; it forbids creditors from garnishing your wages, repossessing your car, starting or continuing foreclosures, suing or even contacting you in any way about the debt.
- **Debtor.** The person who files a bankruptcy petition. When a husband and wife file together, they are joint debtors.
- **Discharge.** An official court order wiping out your debts. If a debt is erased, it is said to be *discharged*. If someone is denied a discharge, none of his or her debts are wiped out.
- **Dismissal of bankruptcy.** A court order that can bring a bankruptcy case to a halt before it runs its course. When that occurs, usually the result of the debtor's ignoring court directives or otherwise abusing the bankruptcy process, all the debts remain and creditors are free to resume their collection efforts, including foreclosures and lawsuits.
- **Exempt property.** Specific assets that you "own" legally and which are part of the bankruptcy process. These assets cannot be attached because of state or federal laws protecting this property from the claims of creditors.
- **Equity.** The difference between the value of an item and the amount of any liens against it. If your house is worth $100,000 and you owe $75,000 on the mortgage, your equity is $25,000 (assuming there are no other liens against the property). Similarly, if your car is worth $5,000 and you owe $2,000, the equity is $3,000.
- **Exceptions to discharge.** Specific debts that are not wiped out.
- **Joint bankruptcy.** A bankruptcy filed by a husband and wife together. As we explained in chapter 2, one spouse does not have to file bankruptcy just because his or her mate does. And married couples don't have to file together. In fact, sometimes it's better to file separately (see the section on jointly held property in chapter 9).
- **Lien.** A charge against property securing payment of a debt.

Common examples are when a lender has a mortgage against your home or holds title to your car.

• **No-asset case.** A Chapter 7 case in which there are no assets available for creditors to take.

• **Personal property.** Anything that is not attached to land. Cars, household goods, bank accounts, and pensions are all examples of personal property. Some states treat mobile homes as personal property; others deem them real property.

• **Petition date.** The date on which a bankruptcy petition is filed. This is a crucial date in bankruptcy. For the most part, debts arising after this date can't be discharged, and property you acquire after this milestone is not subject to your bankruptcy status.

• **Property of the estate.** All the property you own on the petition date, plus a few specific items you acquire after that. In some situations the concept of "ownership" can be quite complicated: You don't lose any property that is not "property of the estate" because the law does not consider that you really own it. By contrast, "exempt property" is property that you legally own and get to keep because of specific state or federal laws protecting it from creditors.

• **Reaffirmation.** A promise to pay a debt in a Chapter 7 bankruptcy that would otherwise be wiped out. You might want to reaffirm the obligation to keep the property that secures the debt to maintain credit privileges.

• **Real property.** Land and the things permanently attached to it, such as buildings, fences, and built-in swimming pools.

• **Redemption.** The right of a Chapter 7 debtor to eliminate a security interest by making a lump sum payment to the secured creditor in an amount equal to the value of the collateral. This concept is especially beneficial with department store credit purchases since the value of the item plummets the moment you walk out the door. In that case you almost always owe more for the item than it is worth.

For example, you may have bought a washer and dryer for $1,000 that is now worth only $300, even though you still owe $850. Redemption allows you to keep the washer and dryer by making a lump sum payment of $300 and wiping out the rest of the debt.

Typically, the value is negotiated or decided by the court. Don't confuse redemption of personal property under the Bankruptcy Code with the state's right of redemption law as it pertains to mortgage foreclosure.

• **Secured debt.** A claim against a particular item of personal or real property (see **Personal property** and **Real property** for an explanation of the differences between the two). If you owe more than the collateral is worth, the amount of the secured debt is limited to the value of the collateral. For example, if your car is worth $3,000 and you owe $4,000, the lender has a secured claim for $3,000.

• **Security interest.** A lien on personal property that you grant to a creditor. Examples: The lender holding the title to your car has a security interest in the vehicle. When you buy an item on a department store charge account, you frequently give the store a security interest in the item.

• **341 meeting.** A meeting you attend with your attorney about forty days after the petition date. It's a session in which a trustee and creditors can ask you questions about your property and debts.

• **Unsecured debt.** A claim that is not tied to any particular item of personal or real property or a claim that is greater than the value of the collateral securing it. The difference between the value of the collateral and the amount you owe is an unsecured debt. Example: Your car is worth $3,000 but you owe $4,000. The balance of the debt, $1,000, is unsecured.

TYPES OF BANKRUPTCY AND ELIGIBILITY

There are five kinds of bankruptcy, identified by their chapter in the Bankruptcy Code.

- Chapter 7: straight bankruptcy
- Chapter 9: municipal bankruptcy
- Chapter 11: business reorganizations
- Chapter 12: family farmer reorganizations
- Chapter 13: consumer and small business reorganizations.

Most consumer debtors file under Chapter 7 or Chapter 13. Chapter 11 is available to individuals but is typically used by business debtors. It's a very complicated and expensive process.

Some consumers qualify as family farmers. If so, they may choose to file under Chapter 12.

Many experts predict that since the 1994 amendments increased the debt limitations for Chapter 13, self-employed persons will discover that Chapter 13 may provide a much better and cheaper way to reorganize their business than Chapter 11.

ELIGIBILITY

Unless you have had a bankruptcy case dismissed within the last 180 days, you are probably eligible for some sort of relief under the Bankruptcy Code.

If you have had a previous bankruptcy dismissed within this period, you still may be eligible, but be sure to tell your lawyer immediately.

Where do you file if you have lived in two or more jurisdictions? That can be a little confusing because each state has at least one judicial district and some have several. The only judicial district where you are eligible to file bankruptcy is the one where you lived the greater portion of the 180 days before the bankruptcy filing. So in some places just moving over county lines could affect where you file.

In addition, each type of bankruptcy also has its own specific eligibility requirement pros and cons.

Chapter 7 Defined

Chapter 7 is what most people think of when they hear the word *bankruptcy*. It is often referred to as *straight bankruptcy*. In this type of bankruptcy all your dischargeable debts are wiped out, there is no repayment plan, and any nonexempt assets you own on the petition date can be sold by the trustee and the proceeds distributed to your creditors.

As a practical matter, the vast majority of consumer bankruptcies are *no-asset cases,* meaning that no property is taken away from the debtor because it's all exempt.

Chapter 7 Eligibility

There are no maximum debt restrictions for Chapter 7, so virtually everyone is eligible for bankruptcy relief.

There is, however, a caveat called *substantial abuse.* In certain instances the court can dismiss a Chapter 7 consumer case if it finds that discharging all debts would be an abuse of the bankruptcy process. That doesn't happen very often and usually only in cases where a debtor earns more than $30,000, has very few expenses, and could pay a large portion of the bills over a short time if he or she were so inclined. Even then, before dismissing a case for substantial abuse, the court will usually provide an opportunity to convert it to a Chapter 13.

If most of your debts are business related, or taxes (which are not considered consumer debts), your case cannot be dismissed for substantial abuse.

Finally, although you would be eligible for a Chapter 7, your bills could not be discharged if you received a discharge in a bankruptcy filed within the the past six years. There is, of course, seldom any point in filing a Chapter 7 if you won't get a discharge. This restriction applies only if you received a discharge in the earlier case. It would not apply, for example, if your earlier case were dismissed.

There's an exception to the prior bankruptcy rule that allows a Chapter 7 discharge within six years if the earlier case was a Chapter 13 and creditors in that case were paid at least 70 percent of their claims.

Chapter 13 Defined

In a Chapter 13 the debtor proposes a debt repayment plan, which, once approved by the court, keeps creditors at bay so long as the debtor continues to make payments.

Most Chapter 13 plans are maintained by regular monthly payments. Before filing, the debtor prepares a monthly budget of estimated income and expenses. The difference between projected income and anticipated expenses is considered *disposable income*. That is the amount you have to pay each month.

> For years, Arthur had contributed 10 percent of his monthly income to his church, but when he filed Chapter 13, the court told him that this money had to be paid to creditors instead. The court thought that it was admirable for Arthur to give to the church, but decided his creditors shouldn't have to subsidize his generosity.

Under most Chapter 13 plans, creditors receive only a small percentage of their claim, and any balance owed after completion of the plan, which ranges from three to five years, is discharged.

The length of your plan is determined by several factors. Every plan must pass two tests: the *best-interest test* and the *best-efforts test*.

• *Best-interest test.* Unsecured creditors must be paid at least as much as they would receive if you filed a Chapter 7 instead of a Chapter 13. If all your property is exempt and unsecured creditors would receive nothing in a Chapter 7, they would also get nothing in a Chapter 13. On the other hand, if you have $5,000 worth of nonexempt property, your plan must propose to pay at least this much.

• *Best-efforts test.* If, like most people, you want to pay unsecured creditors less than 100 percent of their claims, you must pay all of your disposable income into the plan for at least three years. That's not as bad as it sounds; you won't have any extra money, but you will have what you need, including reasonable entertainment expenses. The court probably won't allow you to continue making contributions to your pension plan, however, unless they are required as a condition of your employment. But you're allowed to maintain your home, and maybe even budget for major expenditures, such as a new roof or paint job, if necessary to preserve the property. You won't be allowed to include budget items for unnecessary improvements to your home, however.

The maximum allowable length of a plan is sixty months. (See the budget worksheet in appendix 4 and the appendix 5 worksheet on figuring the length of your Chapter 13 plan.)

Chapter 13 Eligibility

Corporations and partnerships are not eligible for Chapter 13, but individuals with regular income are. It doesn't matter where the income comes from so long as it's stable and regular. The income can come from wages or self-employment or even unemployment benefits.

Unlike Chapter 7, Chapter 13 can be filed even if you had a bankruptcy within the last six years.

There are certain debt limitations, which have been increased by the 1994 amendments. Now, to be eligible for Chapter 13, your unsecured debts must be less than $250,000 and your secured debts less than $750,000. The difference between secured and unsecured debts is discussed under that topic in chapter 4, "Forgive Us Our Trespasses."

Extremely large child-support arrearages or tax obligations could, as a practical matter, make you ineligible for Chapter 13 because these claims must be paid in full over a maximum period of sixty months. If repayment within this period was impossible, there would be little point in filing Chapter 13.

Chapter 13 Pros and Cons

The following advantages of Chapter 13 might outweigh the burden of obligating yourself to a repayment plan:

- Nondischargeable taxes can be paid in installments, without interest or penalties.
- Back alimony and child support can be stretched out and paid over three to five years.
- Back payments on your home or car can be brought current over the life of the plan.
- Car payments can be reduced.
- Certain debts—such as fraud, other intentional wrongdoing, marital property divisions, loans used to pay federal income taxes, and some taxes—can only be discharged in a Chapter 13.
- You can keep nonexempt property.
- The six-year restriction preventing a Chapter 7 discharge does not apply.

Some people claim that a Chapter 13 filing is less detrimental to your credit rating than a Chapter 7, but that remains to be seen. Actually, if you think about it, a person may be a better credit risk after a Chapter 7 because the slate is clean, debts are eliminated, and he or she can't file another Chapter 7 for six years.

Another problem with Chapter 13 bankruptcies is that about two-thirds of them fail, and the debtor winds up in Chapter 7 anyhow.

Chapter 12 Defined

Chapter 12 is a special type of bankruptcy reserved for family farmers. It's important to consider whether you might qualify (see eligibility requirements below).

If you run a family farm, Chapter 12 provides most of the benefits of a Chapter 13, and then some. Repayment plans are not restricted to five years, and there are fewer limitations on the debtor's ability to restructure home mortgages.

The downside of a Chapter 12 is that dischargeable debts are limited to those dischargeable in a Chapter 7. You don't get the "super discharge" available in a Chapter 13.

Chapter 12 Eligibility

Congress thought that family farmers play a unique role in our culture and economy and need special protection.

To qualify as a family farmer, a person must meet each of the following requirements:

- Debts may not exceed $1.5 million.
- Eighty percent of those debts (excluding the home mortgage) must be from farming operations.
- Fifty percent of income from the preceding year must have come from farming operations.

What is a farming operation? Good question. The courts have been trying to figure that out for years, with some peculiar results.

For example, one debtor whose sole income—less than $10,000—for the year before bankruptcy came from cutting and selling firewood from trees grown on his land was held to be a family farmer. As a result, the court approved a repayment plan that actually reduced the mortgage on his home and allowed it to be paid over twenty years. It's something to consider if there is any chance you might qualify.

GETTING PROFESSIONAL HELP

You are best off consulting a lawyer, one who really knows the Bankruptcy Code.

Be wary of "bankruptcy clinics." Some are excellent, providing quality services at low rates. But others rely on a high volume of cases, with nonlawyers assigned to do most of the work.

In any event, definitely avoid bankruptcy "filing services," which are outfits run by nonlawyers who claim that all they do is prepare papers and give no legal advice. In reality they do give advice, and it is frequently bad.

It's such a problem that the 1994 amendments specifically make it easier to sue those outfits when they screw up, and authorize jail sentences for filing mills guilty of deceptive advertising.

Preparing to Meet Your Lawyer

After selecting a lawyer and making an appointment, be sure to mention if any foreclosure proceedings or lawsuits are pending, so that the lawyer's office is aware of potential deadlines and any need for an immediate filing.

A little preparation will make your first meeting with the lawyer more productive.

- If you have student loans, call the creditor and find out when the loan first became due and whether there were any periods during which payments were deferred. Be sure to write down the name of the person providing this information.
- Prepare a monthly budget showing all your income and expenses. (See the budget worksheet in appendix 4.)
- Bring copies of your mortgage, showing the date it was recorded in the county records, and copies of the titles on any financed motor vehicles. In addition, bring copies of any loan documents from any consumer finance company. If you don't already have copies, you can get them from the creditor.
- If you have been served with any court papers, bring them.
- Bring any notices from taxing authorities.
- If you owe back child support or alimony, find out the total amount due, and bring a copy of the separation or divorce decree.

• If you've filed bankruptcy within the last six years, bring all your paperwork from that case.

• Finally, bring a list of your creditors.

Your First Meeting with a Lawyer

You may initially be questioned by a paralegal, but you should definitely be given a chance to meet your lawyer at the initial interview so you can determine whether you want her or him to represent you.

If the lawyer or an assistant tells you something different from the information in this book, don't be afraid to ask questions. You and your lawyer are partners in this. If he or she is offended, or won't take the time to address your questions, find another lawyer.

At the first meeting the lawyer should give you a sense of whether bankruptcy is an appropriate solution to your financial dilemma, and if so, under which chapter. You will probably be given a questionnaire to fill out at home. Some important things to remember:

• Disclose all your property on the questionnaire, even if you consider it worthless.

• Don't transfer any property to keep it out of bankruptcy.

• Don't keep more than the minimum balance on deposit with a bank where you owe money, because the bank may attempt to seize the money once the petition is filed.

• Make sure you don't have any checks outstanding when you file bankruptcy.

• Obtain any tax refund to which you are entitled before filing bankruptcy.

After you complete the questionnaire, return it so that the official filing documents can be prepared. When they are ready, a second meeting must be arranged. At this meeting your lawyer will review the official papers with you, make any corrections, and have you sign these documents.

When everything is signed and you have paid all the fees, the documents will be filed. At that point, the automatic stay goes into effect. (See discussion later in this chapter.)

Attorney Fees and Costs

If you are filing a Chapter 7, you will be expected to pay the attorney's fee and court filing fee upfront, before the bankruptcy is filed. (See chapter 2, "Questions and Answers" for clues on coming up with money to cover bankruptcy fees.) In a Chapter 13 a portion of the fee usually can be deferred and paid through the plan.

The fee in a Chapter 7 is usually a fixed amount covering the routine services up to and including the 341 meeting. (More on this meeting later in the chapter.) In most cases no additional services or fees are required.

There is quite a bit more work involved in a Chapter 13, so it's much harder to establish a flat fee. Consequently, lawyers usually charge a fee based on how much time they are required to spend on your case. Chapter 13 also involves an additional cost: the trustee's commissions. Trustees generally get 7 to 10 percent of the payments you make into the plan.

GROUNDWORK FOR CREDIT REPAIR

Sooner or later you'll need to repair your credit standing, and there are some steps you can take before filing to make life easier down the road.

Many banks will not allow someone who recently filed bankruptcy to open checking accounts. The easy way around this is to open a new account in a bank where you don't owe money, deposit only the minimum balance, and don't use the account until after you file.

Another thing you can do is obtain a new credit card or charge account. On any credit application, be sure to accurately list all your debts, the true value of your assets, and the amount of your income. If you succeed in getting a credit card, don't use it until after you file bankruptcy.

If you don't owe any money on an account, you don't list it in your bankruptcy, so the creditor does not automatically get notice of your bankruptcy. Chances are you will be able to use this account in the future to build up your credit history.

You can accomplish the same objective by paying off an account before you file. But don't pay more than $600. (See the section on preferential transfers in chapter 7, "Games People Play.")

Once you've made the decision to file, your credit reports after bankruptcy will look better if you don't procrastinate. Usually, it's best not to pay bills on the eve of bankruptcy, but note that creditors will continue to report you to credit bureaus up to the time you actually file. These bad reports stay on your credit history after bankruptcy, so it's best to have as few as possible.

AUTOMATIC STAY

The automatic stay, one of the most important benefits of bankruptcy, kicks in the moment your bankruptcy petition is filed. It is a court order forbidding creditors from taking any further action against you or your property without first getting the court's permission.

A creditor who "willfully" violates the stay can be fined and ordered to pay you damages. But there's a catch: a creditor is not subject to punishment unless he or she knows about your bankruptcy, and it usually takes about ten days for the court to get around to mailing official notice to all your creditors.

In theory, most actions taken by a creditor before learning of the bankruptcy can be undone, but this can be a hassle and may cost you attorney fees.

It's not uncommon for a secured creditor to repossess a car after the bankruptcy is filed but before learning of it. Usually, your lawyer can persuade the creditor to return the car voluntarily, but you can't recover damages or attorney fees.

So the moral of the story is: take the initiative and notify certain creditors of your bankruptcy as soon as it is filed. Then, if any of them violate the stay, they have to pay you damages and reimburse your attorney fees. Specifically, be sure to notify creditors who financed your car, any creditor foreclosing against your property, suing you, or garnishing your wages.

• If you are in default on a car loan, be sure to wait until after the bankruptcy is actually filed before notifying the creditor. Otherwise, the creditor might repossess the vehicle immediately before the automatic stay goes into effect.

• If a foreclosure is scheduled, personally attend the sale and announce that you've filed bankruptcy and that the sale cannot lawfully proceed. Bring a copy of your bankruptcy petition in case anyone wants verification.

• Notify anyone who is suing you, and send a copy of your bankruptcy petition to the court.

• Tell your employer, so no more funds are garnished from your pay.

Exceptions to Automatic Stay

The automatic stay is a great benefit, but it doesn't shield you from:

• criminal prosecution
• collection or modification of alimony or child support
• actions by a governmental unit to enforce its regulatory power.

But note that when an action by a governmental unit is an indirect attempt to collect a prepetition debt, the automatic stay *still applies.* For example, many states have laws suspending a person's driver's license if he or she doesn't pay a judgment arising from a car accident. Since the real reason the states take action in such cases is to collect money, these proceedings are not excepted from the automatic stay. By contrast, since medical licensing requirements are designed to protect the public from incompetent doctors, not to collect money, the stay does not stop the state from revoking a doctor's license to practice medicine due to misconduct. It is very doubtful that a physician's license could be lifted simply because he or she filed bankruptcy.

When the state started proceedings to suspend Frank's driver's license for not paying a judgment arising from an accident, his lawyer immediately filed bankruptcy. The automatic stay stopped the license suspension proceedings, and later, when Frank got his bankruptcy discharge, the state had to cancel the proceedings altogether. If Frank's lawyer had waited until the license was actually suspended to file the bankruptcy petition, Frank would have had to wait until his bankruptcy discharge was entered to get his license back.

Bank Accounts

There's nothing a bank hates more than to have to give you the money in your account when you are bankrupting a debt to them. In late 1995, the U.S. Supreme Court held that banks can indeed freeze the account of someone who owes them money.

There is an easy way to avoid the problem: withdraw almost all your money before filing bankruptcy, and deposit it in a bank where you don't owe anything.

Spouses and Relatives

For the most part, the automatic stay protects only the debtor and property of the debtor.

Your bankruptcy will not, for example, stop foreclosure of your mother's house even though you live there. Similarly, your bankruptcy would not prevent repossession of your spouse's car if he or she doesn't also file bankruptcy.

Cosigned Debts

Since the automatic stay is personal, it usually doesn't protect cosigners. If you file bankruptcy on a cosigned debt, the creditor can still go after the other person.

There is, however, an important exception in Chapter 13 cases, and it's known as the *codebtor stay*. Such a stay comes into play when someone cosigned a loan for you but you got the money. Creditors are prevented, temporarily anyhow, from pouncing on the cosigner, and permanently if the Chapter 13 plan proposes to pay the cosigned debt in full. If the Chapter 13 plan doesn't include full repayment of the cosigned debt, the court will eventually allow the creditor to go after your mother-in-law, cousin, or whoever put their credit on the line for you.

341 MEETING

The 341 meeting, named after a section of the Bankruptcy Code, is a session with the trustee and your creditors. You have to attend the meeting with your lawyer and answer questions about documents filed with your petition.

A Chapter 7 trustee will focus on whether you listed all your assets and whether there is any nonexempt property that can be sold for the benefit of creditors.

In a Chapter 13 case the trustee will be more concerned with whether your payment plan meets all the legal requirements and whether you will be able to make all the payments. The budget filed with your petition will be carefully scrutinized.

Creditors are entitled to ask limited questions at the meeting, but they rarely bother to show up. Even if they do attend, creditors can't berate or harass you about the bankruptcy or hassle you about your debts. The 341 meeting is designed for fact-finding, not brow-beating.

In most Chapter 7 cases, once you complete the 341 meeting, the only thing left is the *order of discharge,* which the court automatically issues in about three months.

In Chapter 13 cases there is a second proceeding called a *confirmation hearing,* where the court determines whether or not to confirm your plan. In many states, if the Chapter 13 trustee approves of your plan at the 341 meeting, and if no creditors object to your plan, you do not have to attend the confirmation hearing. The court will approve your plan as a matter of course.

THE PLAYERS

To understand the bankruptcy process, you need to know a little about the players involved.

Bankruptcy Judge

Bankruptcy judges are appointed by the federal court. Chances are that you will never even need to see the bankruptcy judge, who ultimately decides disputes between the other players.

U.S. Trustee

The U.S. trustee is an employee of the U.S. Justice Department. His or her job is to supervise the private trustees, watch for so-called substantial abuse, prosecute bankruptcy fraud, and administer Chapter 11 cases. You probably won't have anything to do with this trustee.

But don't confuse the U.S. trustee with the private trustee, whom you will surely encounter.

Private Trustee

The private trustee is initially appointed by the U.S. trustee. Although creditors can elect a different person at the 341 meeting, they rarely do so.

The private trustee's job is to get whatever assets of yours that he or she can to pay your creditors. For his or her troubles, the trustee, who is not a government employee, is paid a set amount, from your court filing fee, for every case, plus a commission based on any of your assets that can be sold for the benefit of creditors. Keep in mind that the private trustee is not on your side and his or her interests may well be the opposite of yours.

In the past, Chapter 7 trustees would usually treat a case as a no-asset case if there was less than $1,000 in nonexempt assets because the trustee's commission would not cover the amount of extra work required to treat a bankruptcy as an asset case. But the 1994 amendments have increased the trustee's commission from 10 percent to 25 percent, so there's a good chance he or she will be more eager to sell nonexempt assets than in the past. Also note that trustees are always quick to latch on to items that are easy to liquidate, like an income tax refund.

If the Chapter 7 trustee closes your case without selling any properly listed asset, that property is *abandoned*—which means it's yours again. What if it later turns out that the property is more valuable than the trustee thought? Tough beans. This abandonment cannot be undone, and the property is yours to keep.

Private Trustee in Chapter 13. The game is a little different for the Chapter 13 trustee; he or she is paid a commission of up to 10 percent of the plan payments. Although the primary responsibility is to your creditors, the trustee has an interest in seeing your Chapter 13 succeed. Reason: the longer you make payments, the more commission the trustee makes.

THE CLAIMS PROCESS

This section explains the way creditors get their money from bankruptcy cases. You need to read it only if you file: Chapter 13, or if you file Chapter 7 with nonexempt assets and you have nondischargeable debts, especially taxes, alimony, or child support. (Nondischargeable debts are generally those that don't get wiped out in bankruptcy.)

Proof of Claim

A creditor does not receive any money from a bankruptcy unless a paper called a *proof of claim* is filed with the court. Most creditors have 90 days from the 341 meeting to file such a claim. If a creditor doesn't file one, the debtor may lodge a proof of claim on behalf of the creditor up to 120 days from the 341 meeting.

The 1994 amendments give special treatment to governmental units, allowing them 180 days after the petition date to file a proof of claim. It's unclear how long a debtor has to file proof of claim if the government doesn't.

Sometimes it's important that a particular creditor receive payment from the bankruptcy trustee, and your attorney should file a proof of claim on behalf of the creditor just to be sure.

In a Chapter 13 you want to make sure that a proof is filed on behalf of secured claims being paid through the plan. Secured claims will be explained in detail later on, but in general they refer to creditors who have collateral, such as your car, that they can take in lieu of cash.

In most jurisdictions the Chapter 13 trustee sends debtors a summary of all the claims that have been filed. You should go over this carefully, and if you disagree with any of the claims contact your lawyer, so that an objection can be filed.

In a Chapter 7 case you need to ensure that any assets are used to pay debts that would linger after bankruptcy. Especially debts for taxes, alimony, and child support, which are *priority claims*. This means they get paid first, before any money is distributed to other creditors.

An experienced lawyer would have told Skinflint Homer to postpone his bankruptcy for a month, so his student loan could be wiped out. And the lawyer would have known enough to file under Chapter 13, so Homer could have paid off his taxes without interest or penalties, and on a schedule he could afford. It might have cost Homer another $200 to hire an attorney, but he would have saved that amount many times over in the long run. And there's a good chance he would have been able to keep his fishing boat.

4

. . . .

FORGIVE US
OUR TRESPASSES

Annette, a single mother of twin toddlers struggling to make ends meet on a schoolteacher's salary, was at wit's end. After putting it off for months, she finally went in for the hysterectomy she needed—and the doctor botched the job so badly that she couldn't go back to work. Her credit cards were maxed out. The hospital still wanted ten grand, bill collectors were threatening to sue, and her car was about to be repossessed. Annette had a pending medical malpractice lawsuit, but a pending claim doesn't pay the bills. Her remedy: bankruptcy.

Bankruptcy is frequently the only, not just the best, route to financial freedom. However, not all debts are treated the same in bankruptcy, and some, called *nondischargeable debts,* may continue to haunt you. Others, the so-called secured debts, require special nurturing. And to further complicate matters, Congress and the courts have established different rules for debts in Chapter 13 and Chapter 7.

This chapter puts everything in perspective. It highlights:

- the difference between secured and unsecured debts
- the difference between dischargeable and nondischargeable debts
- the common types of nondischargeable debts
- which debts are dischargeable in a Chapter 13 but not in a Chapter 7
- the difference between having just a single debt excepted from discharge and having none of your debts discharged.

SECURED AND UNSECURED DEBTS

If creditors can't get your money, what can they get? The answer is: anything you put up, maybe unwittingly, to guarantee your payments. If a creditor has collateral, the debt is secured. It's as simple as that.

Mortgages

People commonly think in terms of the bank's giving them a mortgage to buy a house. Actually, you gave the bank a mortgage. That means if the debt—or any debt secured by the property—isn't paid, you may lose the house through foreclosure (unless you are shielded by various bankruptcy provisions, of course). It's exactly the same deal when the lender holds the title to your car.

Department Store Charges

When you buy items on credit at certain department stores, you probably don't realize it but you agree that whatever you bought is collateral for a secured account. Where does the store get the authority to do this? From you. It's right there in the fine print on credit documents nobody bothers to read before signing.

The bottom line is that if you fall behind in your payments to any of these stores, the store can take back any items you bought on credit.

Consumer Loan Companies

When you borrow money from one of those companies that specialize in making small loans to consumers, you may be required to give the lender a security interest in all your earthly belongings. In theory, if you don't pay, the lender can get a court order seizing all of these assets and selling enough of them to pay the debt.

In practice, this is rarely done; the value of most people's stuff does not justify the expense involved in seizing and selling this kind of property. Rather obviously, the companies are looking for leverage. They figure that if they can threaten to take everything you own, you'll find a way to pay them. They are often right, although frequently they don't have a legal leg to stand on. Such blanket security interests can be canceled in bankruptcy.

Credit Cards, Medical Bills, Etc.

Most debts, including medical bills and those on major credit cards such as Visa, MasterCard, and Discover, are unsecured. So are most mail-order accounts. As a result, the creditor can't take any of your property if the bills aren't paid.

Secured and Unsecured at the Same Time

It sounds like something from George Orwell or Yogi Berra, but the same debt can be both secured and unsecured. In bankruptcy, a debt is considered secured only to the extent of the value of the collateral.

Let's say your car has a value of $2,000 and you owe $3,000. Under the Bankruptcy Code the creditor has two claims: (1) a secured claim equal to the value of the collateral, $2,000; (2) an unsecured claim for the $1,000 balance.

By contrast, if your home has a market value of $75,000, and you owe $50,000, the whole claim is secured because the value of the collateral, $75,000, is at least as much as the $50,000 debt. (More on this in chapter 9, "Home Sweet Home.")

By the way, the value of an asset is the amount you would receive if you sold it, not what it would cost to replace it. When you file bankruptcy, you are required to list the value of each asset. If the trustee or a creditor disagrees, and you can't reach an agreement, the court decides how much it's worth.

Dragnet Clauses

A *dragnet clause* enables the lender to make an end run around what is seemingly an unsecured loan. Here's how it works: Many lenders stick such a clause in their contracts, stating that any collateral they have secures every loan that you owe them. So if, for example, you borrowed some cash from ABC Loan Company and, in a separate transaction, financed your car or home with this firm, the vehicle or house could be in jeopardy unless you agree to pay back the loans.

Traditionally, courts allowed finance companies to get away with this gimmickry. More recently, however, some courts have frowned on dragnet clauses and refused to enforce the contract. If you have more than one loan with any lender, it is imperative that your lawyer examine the contracts for dragnet clauses.

DISCHARGEABLE DEBTS

It's a good idea to carefully decide not only whether you should file bankruptcy but when. Generally, any bills you owe at the time you file will be eliminated. Also generally, debts that "arise" (see below) after that are not.

Simple? Sort of.

Debts "arise" when the events causing the liability occur, even though an actual claim is not made until later. For example, when you buy something on credit, the debt arises at that moment, even though the bill may not come due for a month.

Oftentimes, people discover that they filed bankruptcy too soon. For example, if someone filed bankruptcy before undergoing extensive medical treatment, the medical bills resulting from this treatment wouldn't be included in the bankruptcy. But be careful about racking up bills after deciding to file bankruptcy. If the creditor can prove you didn't intend to pay the debt, it won't be wiped out in Chapter 7.

Secured Debts Are Dischargeable

Most secured debts are dischargeable, but if you choose to discharge this kind of debt you would have to give up the property securing the obligation.

For example, you could discharge your home mortgage, but if you did, you'd lose your home. Same with a car that's financed. Fortunately, you usually have the choice of not discharging these debts and keeping the collateral. But that doesn't necessarily mean you have to pay the whole debt in order to keep the collateral.

Frequently, when the collateral is worth less than the debt, you need only pay its value. In a Chapter 13 you can even pay this amount over time.

NONDISCHARGEABLE DEBTS

Certain types of debts are decreed nondischargeable under specific sections of the Bankruptcy Code, regardless of whether they are tied to specific property. These debts are discussed below.

Income Taxes

Usually, taxes are not discharged in a Chapter 7 and must be paid in full during the life of a Chapter 13. But under a very complicated set of rules and court decisions, you might be able to escape paying income taxes if enough time passes before you file bankruptcy.

Differences in Chapter 7 and Chapter 13. Generally, if you filed a nonfraudulent return but weren't able to pay the taxes, the debt to Uncle Sam can be discharged in either Chapter 7 or Chapter 13 if this debt is more than three years old, counting from the date the return was due. But the ground rules can be quite different in Chapter 7 and Chapter 13.

For example, if a tax return for 1989 was due April 15, 1990, you might reasonably think the three-year period started on that date. But various events can interrupt the three years and actually add more time. For instance:

• If you had an earlier bankruptcy case, the time your case was open is not counted and six months are added to the three years.

• If you got an extension of time to file your return, the three years would run from the date the extension expired, not the date the return was originally due.

• Any time period a Taxpayer Assistance Order is in effect does not count. See the section entitled "Taxpayer Ombudsman" in chapter 13 for more information on Taxpayer Assistance Orders.

If you neglected to file a return, filed it late, submitted a fraudulent return, or otherwise tried to evade taxes, life is more complicated.

If you didn't file a return at all, the taxes are not dischargeable in a Chapter 7, no matter how old they are. Although the IRS can, and often will, file a *dummy return*—which is a return filed by the feds in your name so the government can assess a tax—that won't get you off the hook.

Additionally, if you filed late, the taxes would not be dischargeable in a Chapter 7 unless two years passed between the filing of the late return and the bankruptcy petition. Example: Your 1991 income tax return was due on April 15, 1992. But you didn't actually file the return until July 21, 1993, so the taxes would not be dischargeable in a Chapter 7 filed before July 21, 1995.

With a fraudulent return, the clock never starts running. If you intentionally evaded taxes, the Chapter 7 is not going to do you any good, at least on that issue.

Things are different in a Chapter 13 bankruptcy. Taxes more than three years old may be discharged even if you never filed a return, filed a fraudulent return, or willfully tried to evade the taxes. In fact, many times it's better to file a Chapter 13 before filing delinquent income tax returns. Regardless, you should still have the return ready to file as soon as you file your bankruptcy petition, for two prime reasons:

• You need to know the amount of any nondischargeable taxes in order to prepare a Chapter 13 plan.

• The IRS routinely checks Chapter 13 filers to ensure that such debtors have completed all necessary tax returns. If you haven't filed all your returns, the IRS may get a court order requiring you to file within a very short period, like fifteen days. The penalty for missing that deadline is severe: the Chapter 13 case is dismissed.

Assessment. There's an additional requirement for getting rid of taxes in either a Chapter 7 or a Chapter 13. The taxes must have been assessed more then 240 days before the bankruptcy was filed.

Figuring out just when the taxes were assessed, however, is complicated and tricky. In general, if the taxes are otherwise dischargeable, they have usually been assessed for enough time—unless they were imposed after an audit of your return or after the IRS filed a dummy return.

Interest and Penalties. There are two time periods to be concerned with here, prepetition and postpetition.

Prepetition interest is, for the most part, treated the same as the tax; if the tax is nondischargeable, so is the interest.

In a Chapter 7 the same goes for prepetition penalties, unless the transaction giving rise to the penalties occurred more than three years before bankruptcy. In a Chapter 13, however, prepetition penalties are discharged even if the tax is not.

Postpetition interest on unsecured, nondischargeable taxes continues to accrue during and after a Chapter 7 case, but not in a Chapter 13. Yet, if the Chapter 13 is dismissed or converted to Chapter 7, interest is added as if there had been no bankruptcy.

Postpetition penalties on nondischargeable taxes are not assessed while either a Chapter 7 or a Chapter 13 case is open—but a Chapter 7 case is usually not open very long, typically just for a few months.

Federal Tax Liens and IRS Threats. If the IRS records a *Notice of Tax Lien* before you file bankruptcy, the above rules do not apply and it becomes even more difficult to discharge taxes. If you suspect that a tax lien is about to be filed, contact a bankruptcy specialist IMMEDIATELY.

Sometimes collection agents will use dire threats to try to get you to sign papers waiving various time limits. Don't do it without first getting professional advice.

Payment of Nondischargeable Taxes over Time. Even if the income taxes aren't old enough to be discharged, you can still pay them over three to five years in a Chapter 13 and, if no Notice of Tax Lien has been filed, without interest or penalties provided the IRS agrees.

While you are in Chapter 13, the IRS can't bug you about prepetition taxes and it can't file a Notice of Tax Lien.

Postpetition Taxes. Postpetition taxes are not suspended during a bankruptcy case, but in a Chapter 13 the plan can be amended to allow them to be paid over time.

Another way to handle postpetition taxes is to submit a payment proposal to the IRS when you file your return. If you propose to pay the postpetition tax within three years, the IRS will probably go along.

Paying Taxes Before Bankruptcy. If you have nondischargeable taxes, consider selling nonexempt property and paying off the tax debt before filing bankruptcy. If you voluntarily pay taxes before bankruptcy, you can force the IRS to apply the payments to nondischargeable taxes. You lose this option once you file bankruptcy. See chapter 13, "Debt Free Without Bankruptcy," for a further discussion of the benefits of allocating tax payments. But there are some traps here (see the section on preferential transfers in chapter 7, "Games People Play"), so don't pay any taxes without first consulting with your lawyer.

Statute of Limitations. If taxes are old enough, they might be barred by the statute of limitations. If so, the taxes and any tax lien will disappear even when you don't file bankruptcy.

Generally, the statute of limitations on federal taxes is ten years from the date of assessment. But that time period can be extended under certain circumstances:

• An IRS collection agent intimidates you into signing a written waiver of the statute of limitations.

• If you file bankruptcy during the ten-year period, the time that the case is open, plus an additional six months, is added to the ten-year period.

• If you make a formal *offer in compromise* to the IRS (offering to settle the tax liability by paying only a portion of the total obligation), the time the IRS spends considering the proposal is added to the ten-year period, plus another year just for good measure.

• If you successfully obtain a *Taxpayer Assistance Order*, the time that this order is in effect is added to the ten years.

Keep in mind that the clock doesn't start running—ever—until you file a tax return.

If the IRS hasn't bothered you for years, then all of a sudden comes down like a load of bricks, chances are good that the statute of limitations is about to expire and the agency is trying to pressure you into agreeing to extend it. Don't let the IRS intimidate you; see a lawyer. Right now.

Often, the IRS will make a determination that it's just not worth pursuing you right now, because you don't have anything it wants to take. So the IRS classifies your account as "uncollectible" and checks back every couple of years to see if your financial situation has improved.

Tax Protesters. The IRS is not particularly fond of protesters—nor are the courts—and if you have a history of opposing income taxes on constitutional grounds, or any grounds, it is probably going to try to make a public example out of you.

No, it doesn't mean a public flogging. But it does mean the IRS is going to strenuously object to the discharging of old taxes in Chapter 7, under a rule that taxes you willfully tried to evade don't get discharged, or Chapter 13, using a "bad faith" allegation.

State Income Taxes. For the most part, the same rules that apply to federal taxes also cover state income taxes. However, there are some things you need to watch out for.

Most, if not all, states require that you file an amended state return if your federal tax liability for that year has been changed (perhaps as a result of an audit). Some courts hold that if a taxpayer fails to file an amended state return in this situation, his or her initial state return is deemed "unfiled." The result is that the entire tax, not just the amount that would have been added had you amended the state return, can no longer be discharged in Chapter 7.

Other Taxes

As a general rule, nonincome taxes (which are not trust fund taxes; see below) are dischargeable in Chapter 7 or Chapter 13 if whatever caused the tax liability occurred more than three years before the bankruptcy filing date.

Business Taxes. If you or a business you controlled ever had an employee, you were required to withhold certain taxes from her or his salary and pay them to the government on a quarterly basis. These are referred to as *trust fund taxes.* These taxes are not dischargeable in any type of bankruptcy unless they are barred by the statute of limitations.

Sales Taxes. In some states, sales taxes are considered excise taxes and treated like income taxes. In others, they are considered trust fund taxes. So the specific rules vary depending on where you live.

Real Property Taxes. Real property taxes—taxes paid on a home, land, or other real estate—are dischargeable, assuming that you don't intend to keep the property. Reason: real property taxes are typically assessed against the property but not against the owner personally.

Personal Property Taxes. Personal property taxes—taxes paid on items that are not real estate, like cars—are not dischargeable if, under local law, they were assessed against the owner personally rather than just the property.

Loans to Pay Taxes

Under the 1994 amendments, debts incurred to pay nondischargeable federal (but not state) taxes are also nondischargeable in Chapter 7. If you pay federal taxes before bankruptcy, be ready to show that you didn't use borrowed funds.

Student Loans

A student loan is not dischargeable in either a Chapter 7 or a Chapter 13 unless it is more than seven years old or repayment would impose an "undue hardship" (see below) on you.

Nondischargeable student loans include regular government-guaranteed loans as well as tuition owed directly to nonprofit educational institutions, or to nonprofit lenders that fund student loan programs. Surprisingly, they also include loans for tuition to private trade schools, like truck driver or mechanic training courses, if, as is often the case, the loans are guaranteed by a governmental unit.

In 1990 an amendment to the Bankruptcy Code expanded the definition of student loan to include "educational benefits" provided by nonprofit institutions. Since then, courts have had to decide whether debts for books, supplies, student housing, and the like are educational benefits. As you would expect, they have come to different conclusions.

> Barb was lucky the day she was turned down for a guaranteed student loan to attend truck driving school. Lucky? Sure thing. She had to borrow money directly from the school—a debt that could be discharged in bankruptcy.

Courts disagree on whether credit unions are nonprofit lenders. Student loans to these outfits have been wiped out in some cases but not in others.

Cosigners. Student loans are not dischargeable even if you are only a cosigner. If you cosigned for your child's student loan, not only are you liable if he or she doesn't pay, but this obligation can't be wiped out in bankruptcy.

Computing the Time Period. When counting the seven years, you start from the date the first payment was due, usually six months after you leave school. You must subtract any period during which payments were deferred or any period of a prior bankruptcy.

Before talking to a bankruptcy specialist, you should call the holder of the student loan and find out these dates. Be sure to write down the name of the person providing this information.

Consolidation Loans. Don't let the holder of your student loans entice you into consolidating all the loans into one new student loan. That will start the seven-year period running all over again.

Undue Hardship. Even if the student loan is not seven years old, you can discharge all or a part of it by convincing a court that special circumstances exist that would impose "undue hardship" on you or your family if you had to repay this loan. This is very difficult to do, and few debtors are successful.

You will have to convince the court that you:

- really tried your best to pay the loan
- did everything possible to maximize your income and minimize your expenses
- wouldn't be able to survive at a poverty-level standard of living if required to repay the loan.

When considering whether repaying the loan would constitute an undue hardship, some courts are willing to consider whether you received any "benefit" from the education. Most, however, don't care whether your education was cost-effective. Your chances of succeeding on this point are pretty slim if you filed bankruptcy primarily to escape a student loan.

Everyone's financial situation fluctuates, so timing can be critical.

In considering undue hardship, the court must try to predict your future income and expenses, based on your present situation. Obviously, it is best to ask the court to discharge the student loan when your financial situation is at its bleakest. You can ask the court to discharge your student loans even after your bankruptcy case has been closed.

Sammy suffered from chronic fatigue syndrome, which made it very difficult for him to work. The court wasn't about to wipe out his entire student loan, but it did chop the loan in half and made the creditor accept a repayment plan for the balance.

Paying the Loan over Time. If a student loan is not dischargeable, you can still force the creditor to accept payments in an amount you can afford to make through a Chapter 13 plan. But if a nondischargeable student loan is not paid in full during the Chapter 13, you'll still have to pay the rest when your case is over, and interest on the loan balance continues to accrue during the bankruptcy.

There is a hitch, however. If your student loan is one of many debts, it would be nice if you could propose a Chapter 13 plan where the student loan is paid off in full and all other debts are paid much less, but most courts frown on that maneuver and won't allow it.

One ploy that has been effective is commonly known as "Chapter 20," or Chapter 7 + Chapter 13. (There is no Chapter 20 in the Bankruptcy Code.) The strategy is to first file a Chapter 7 to discharge all debts other than the student loan, then file a Chapter 13 case proposing to pay the entire student loan. There's no discrimination problem because you now have only one debt left; the others were discharged in the Chapter 7.

Making Up and Resuming Regular Payments. If the remaining term of the student loan is longer than three years, you could propose to make up all the missed payments on the student loan over the life of a Chapter 13 plan and resume regular monthly payments. Of course, the balance remaining when your Chapter 13 is completed will still have to be paid.

Medical School Loans. Yes, even doctors sometimes go broke.

Loans under the Health Education Assistance Loan (HEAL) program and repayment obligations under scholarships granted by the National Health Services Corporation (NHSC) program are extremely difficult to discharge in bankruptcy.

There is a waiting period that must be satisfied, and a court must decide that requiring repayment would be "unconscionable."

The time period is seven years for HEAL loans and five years for NHSC obligations. Both are measured from the date the obligation first became due to the date of the bankruptcy discharge. (By contrast, the seven-year period for other student loans is measured from the date the obligation first became due to the date of the bankruptcy filing.)

Debts Arising from Fraud or Other Misconduct

Fraudulent debts are not dischargeable in a Chapter 7, but may be in a Chapter 13. In addition, there are specific rules for fines and other court-imposed sanctions.

Charges on the Eve of Bankruptcy. Judges and the court system aren't particularly fond of people who go out and accumulate new debts after deciding to file bankruptcy. Whether you mean it this way or not, it is going to appear as though you racked up a debt without any intention of paying. Don't risk it.

Luxury purchases and credit card cash advances are presumed to be fraudulent if they are made within sixty days of bankruptcy and total more than $1,000. (Obviously, it's not a good idea to put bankruptcy attorney fees on your credit card.)

Just before bankruptcy, Byron racked up nearly $100,000 on his twenty-six credit cards and became the proud owner of a big-screen TV, a powerhouse computer, a state-of-the-art stereo, and dozens of other high-priced toys. Since he was on disability at the time, it wasn't too hard for the court to figure out that Byron never intended to pay those debts. The court refused to discharge them.

In a few cases, courts have also found fraud where debtors ran up credit card bills way beyond their ability to pay.

Joint Credit Cards. Many couples make the mistake of forgetting to cancel joint credit cards when they split up, only to later discover that they are legally responsible for debts they didn't make. Fortunately, the innocent partner may wipe out his or her obligation to pay these charges in bankruptcy, even if the other partner used the card fraudulently.

False Financial Statements. Did you ever wonder why lenders require a complicated financial statement even though you own only a few items? Simple: debts obtained with a false written financial statement are not dischargeable in Chapter 7.

Some lenders will get you to fill out the statement and even encourage you to exaggerate your income or the value of assets. Then, if you ever file bankruptcy, they'll dig out the financial statement and, if they can find any mistakes, claim that their debt is not dischargeable. Sneaky, huh?

The courts think so, and fortunately they require the creditor to prove that you intentionally lied and that the creditor relied on the misrepresentation in making the loan.

But still be on your guard whenever a lender asks for a financial statement. Be scrupulously honest, and don't let anyone coax you into exaggerating. That person may be setting a trap.

Bad Checks. Writing bad checks is considered fraudulent only if the creditor can prove that you knew, or should have known, that the check would bounce.

Most creditors won't bother unless the check is large. So, as a practical matter, debts from rubber checks are frequently discharged.

But don't let a creditor talk you into signing a postdated check. If it turns out that you can't cover the check, the creditor may claim you knew the check was bad, and therefore the debt should not be wiped out; or even worse, the creditor may file criminal bad-check charges against you.

Welfare and Unemployment Benefits. If the bankruptcy court is convinced that you fraudulently obtained social security, unemployment, welfare, or other government benefits, your obligation to repay them would not be discharged in Chapter 7.

Other Wrongdoing. Liabilities from other types of misconduct are also nondischargeable in Chapter 7. These include theft, embezzlement, and injuries you intentionally inflicted on someone or on his or her property.

Default Judgments. If someone sues you claiming that you're guilty of fraud or other misconduct, see a lawyer immediately. If you do nothing, a default judgment can be entered against you and a legal doctrine known as *collateral estoppel* could prevent you from later claiming you were innocent.

Fines

For the most part, fines owed to governmental units can be discharged in Chapter 7 if they are more than three years old, but they can't be discharged in Chapter 13 regardless of their age. But beware! Some courts have decided that it's okay to revoke probation and toss people in jail for discharging fines in a bankruptcy. The courts have not been consistent here, so check out the policy in your own jurisdiction. You don't want to find yourself in the middle of a power struggle between criminal court and bankruptcy court.

Federal Criminal Fines. Fines imposed by a federal court as part of a criminal sentence are in a class by themselves. They follow you for twenty years, constitute a lien against all your property, and can't be discharged in any type of bankruptcy. This special treatment applies only to fines imposed by criminal prosecutions, not civil lawsuits— even if brought by a government agency.

Restitution

If you were convicted of a crime and ordered to pay restitution to the victim, that obligation is not dischargeable in Chapter 13. Because of a loophole in the law, however, a restitution sentence imposed by a state (but not federal) court might be dischargeable in Chapter 7 if the offending conduct occurred more than three years before your bankruptcy.

But, once again, beware! Even though the financial obligation might be wiped out, you could be subject to resentencing in the criminal court and possibly face incarceration.

Drunk-Driving Injuries

If you get drunk or high and injure someone in a car accident, you are going to pay for any personal damages. Liabilities for injuries caused by operation of a motor vehicle while under the influence of alcohol, drugs, or other substances cannot be discharged in either Chapter 7 or Chapter 13.

Alimony, Child Support, and Property Division

When a couple gets divorced, there are generally two related financial issues. The first is whether one spouse is going to pay alimony and child support to cover future expenses. The second is how to divide property.

Unpaid alimony and support obligations are not dischargeable in Chapter 7 or Chapter 13. And, under the 1994 amendments, these obligations must be paid in full during the life of any Chapter 13 case. Obligations arising from property divisions are dischargeable in Chapter 13, but, under the 1994 amendments, are not dischargeable in Chapter 7 unless the bankruptcy court deems them an undue burden on you or your family or decides that the benefit to you of discharging the obligations outweighs the harm that discharge will cause your ex-spouse or child.

If it is not absolutely clear whether payments under a marital settlement agreement or divorce decree are for support or a division of property, many courts will come down on the side of nondischargeable support. If you were ordered to pay your ex-spouse's attorney fees, many judges will do mental backflips to hold the obligation nondischargeable.

Other Divorce Debts

If bankruptcy appears on the horizon, don't agree to pay debts held jointly by you and your ex-spouse. You may unwittingly transform an ordinary dischargeable debt into one that won't go away in bankruptcy.

Here's what could happen:

Say you and your ex-spouse have a joint debt to XYZ Credit Company. As part of the divorce, you assume full responsibility for the debt in an attempt to relieve your ex-spouse from liability.

One of the problems with this approach is that XYZ is not a party to this agreement and doesn't have to go along, even if your promise is included in the state divorce decree.

So when you file bankruptcy, XYZ can still go after your ex-spouse, who will then claim that you have to pay the bill because it's really in the nature of nondischargeable support. Some courts would even let XYZ "step into the shoes" of your ex-spouse and come after you directly, despite your bankruptcy.

Condominium and Cooperative Fees

Folks who live in a condo or co-op are assessed fees to maintain common areas. In most cases these fees are secured by the property and must be paid.

If you intend to keep your residence, simply continue to pay these fees, just as you would taxes or your mortgage.

But if you intend to surrender your residence, beware of falling into a trap. Remember that debts arising after the petition date are not discharged? Well, under the 1994 amendments, condominium or cooperative fees assessed against your property after the petition date are nondischargeable if you continue to live in the property or rent it out after the petition date. So if you intend to surrender a condo or co-op, consider moving out before filing or as soon thereafter as possible.

Borrowing Money to Pay Nondischargeable Debts

Most loans are dischargeable. So, what if you took out a bank loan or a cash advance on your credit card to pay a nondischargeable debt and then turned right around and filed bankruptcy on the new loan?

Bad idea.

If the lender could prove that this was your plan all along, the new loan would not be discharged in Chapter 7, because of fraud, and could be grounds for dismissing any Chapter 13 case on "bad faith" grounds.

Also, as we will discuss in detail (see "Preferential Transfers" in chapter 7, "Games People Play"), the trustee can recover some kinds of payments made before bankruptcy, so she or he can distribute the funds among all your creditors. And remember that under the 1994 amendments, loans to pay federal income taxes are not discharge-able in Chapter 7, even if you weren't planning to file bankruptcy when you took out the loan.

Unscheduled Debts

You should assume that any debts that you fail to list correctly on your bankruptcy schedules will not get discharged, so be very care-ful to list every creditor and provide correct addresses.

Some courts say that in a no-asset Chapter 7 case the unlisted debt is still wiped out, whereas in an asset case or a Chapter 13 it is not. But don't count on it.

Sixty-Day Bar Date. No, this is not about meeting your friends for a couple of drinks, but it could give you a reason to celebrate.

If the basis of a possible nondischargeability claim is fraud, will-ful or malicious conduct, or a marital property division (but not al-imony or support), the creditor has only sixty days from the 341 meeting to file papers with the bankruptcy court asking that the debt not be discharged. If the creditor misses this deadline, the debt is dis-charged.

This is another reason to be careful to list all your creditors. All courts, even those that say unlisted debts get wiped out in no-asset cases, hold that the sixty-day bar date does not apply to unlisted creditors.

The sixty-day bar date applies only in Chapter 7 because the types of debts affected by the bar date are wiped out in Chapter 13 anyway.

Adding Unscheduled Creditors. In a Chapter 7 case it's easy to add an unlisted creditor while your bankruptcy case is still open, but once it is closed, you have to get permission from the court to reopen your case so that the creditor can be added. While the courts usually allow the case to be reopened, there are no guarantees.

In a Chapter 13 case any unlisted creditors should be added within ninety days of the 341 meeting, or else the debt won't be covered by your discharge.

TRACKING DOWN ALL YOUR CREDITORS

If you are not sure of all your creditors, you can start by obtaining copies of your credit reports. There are three nationwide credit-reporting agencies:

- Trans Union (800) 851-2674
- TRW (800) 392-1122
- CBI/Equifax (800) 685-1111

You can call these companies for instructions on how to order your credit report.

Of the three, only the TRW reports include the addresses of your creditors. In addition, TRW offers one free credit report annually.

But remember, the only creditors who will appear on the credit report are those who have reported you. These generally include credit card companies, major department stores, and other large institutional creditors. Smaller creditors, like your doctor, landlord, or local stores, probably don't report to the credit bureaus, at least not until the account is turned over to a collection agency.

Some creditors may report to one or two of the credit bureaus, but usually not all three. So it's not enough to order a credit report from just one company.

This is where "The Confidential Credit Report" comes in. It combines the information from the other credit bureaus into a single report. You can call Credco, the company that compiles these reports, at (800) 443-9342 for ordering instructions. Unfortunately, the report does not include creditors' addresses.

Free Credit Reports

Although TRW offers one free credit report per year, additional reports, and reports from Trans Union or CBI/Equifax, cost $8 each.

If you were denied credit because of a bad report, you can get a free copy by requesting one within thirty days of being turned down.

Sometimes, people apply for a loan knowing they will be turned down in order to get a free copy of their credit report. But they get only a copy of the report used to deny the loan, not all three documents.

REAFFIRMATION

Reaffirmation is a process in which you agree to pay all or part of a debt that would otherwise be wiped out in bankruptcy. It's as if you never filed bankruptcy on that debt; the creditor has all the remedies available before bankruptcy, and can sue you or repossess collateral.

In the old days, creditors used a number of ploys to trick people into reaffirming their debts. In some places, if a debtor merely acknowledged the existence of the discharged debt, it was automatically revived.

The Bankruptcy Code adopted in 1978 finally put an end to those shenanigans by requiring that reaffirmation agreements be in writing, filed with the court, and subject to cancellation by the debtors for sixty days. In addition, the court must conclude, based on information from the debtor or the debtor's attorney, that reaffirmation does not impose an undue hardship and is in the debtor's best interest.

Reasons to Reaffirm

Why on earth would someone file Chapter 7 to wipe out his or her debts and then turn around and reaffirm?

Good question. The most common reasons are:

- to maintain credit privileges
- to compromise a debt to a creditor who claims to have grounds that the debt is nondischargeable anyway
- to keep collateral that secures the debt.

If you are in default on a secured loan, on the day you file under Chapter 7 you must either reaffirm the loan or redeem (we'll discuss *redemption* in more detail in chapter 7, "Games People Play") the collateral in order to keep it.

In some states, if you are current on a secured debt when you filed bankruptcy, you can continue to make future payments without reaffirming the debt. That's a good deal because you just have to continue making postpetition payments so long as you want to keep the collateral. Down the road, if you decide that you no longer want to keep the collateral, you can simply surrender it to the creditor and you won't be responsible for any deficiency.

Creditors, however, hate it when consumers keep goods without agreeing to pay the full amount of the loan, and some courts insist that debtors actually sign a reaffirmation agreement on the loan or redeem the collateral if they want to keep it.

Changing Your Mind

If you sign a reaffirmation agreement, you have the right to change your mind if you give written notice to the creditor within sixty days after it is filed with the court.

Many creditors forget to file reaffirmation agreements with the court, so this is the first thing to check if the creditor tries to sue you on a reaffirmation agreement in the future. If the agreement was never filed with the court, you can still cancel it.

DENIAL OF DISCHARGE

So far, we have been describing certain types of debts that don't get discharged in bankruptcy. There is something much worse: the bankruptcy court has the power to deny your discharge altogether, in which case none of your debts get erased.

This is the ultimate bankruptcy bummer: you have surrendered any nonexempt property, have a bankruptcy on your record, and still owe all your debts. To make matters worse, you can never file Chapter 7 on these debts.

Grounds for Denial of Discharge

A discharge can be denied for:

- intentionally failing to list an asset on your bankruptcy schedules
- intentionally giving false information in your schedules
- lying to the trustee at the 341 meeting
- refusing to cooperate with the trustee
- disobeying an order of the bankruptcy court

- fraudulently transferring property within one year before bankruptcy
- being too aggressive in converting nonexempt assets into exempt assets (see chapter 5, "What Do You Have to Lose?" particularly the section on exemption planning).

Protect Your Discharge

To ensure that you receive a discharge, be completely truthful and make a full disclosure to your lawyer before you file. If you put property in someone else's name, money into someone else's bank account, or otherwise tried to protect any assets from creditors, be sure to tell your lawyer.

These things usually can be repaired if action is taken before you file bankruptcy. It might be too late afterward, so it's very dangerous to remain silent and hope that no one finds out about these transfers. Don't risk it.

Your lawyer should give you copies of all the schedules filed with the bankruptcy court. Review them to make sure that all your assets are listed. Innocent mistakes can easily be fixed, provided you point them out before the 341 meeting. If someone else points out the omitted asset, you may have trouble claiming that the omission was an inadvertent error.

The good news is that courts rarely deny a discharge, and that when denials do occur, it is usually in cases of obvious misrepresentation or refusal to cooperate. If you are completely truthful with your lawyer right from the beginning, he or she can give you a pretty good idea if there is any danger of your discharge being denied.

> Annette made out beautifully. In bankruptcy, all her debts were eliminated, except the car loan. Additionally, Annette's honesty and intelligence in listing the possible malpractice suit on her bankruptcy petition paid off. The trustee didn't bother with the potential award, although you can be sure he would have if he caught her trying to hide it. After bankruptcy, Annette settled with the doctor—for $25,000—and was able to keep every cent. Annette and the twins are doing great!

5

. . . .

WHAT DO YOU
HAVE TO LOSE?

The kids were gone and the mortgage was paid off, so Lance decided to leave the ad agency where he'd toiled for thirty years and retire to Florida. He sold the house in Buffalo, New York, for $215,000 and put the money toward a new home in Daytona Beach. But after six months, Lance was broke. He claimed a *homestead exemption*, a legal perk protecting homes from creditors. Nevertheless, his creditors took him to court, arguing that if Lance hadn't sold his Buffalo home, it could have been used to pay off debts.

So far, we've discussed what you can gain from bankruptcy. Now we tell you what you might lose. This chapter:

- provides more information about which assets are considered property of the estate
- illustrates the role that exemptions play in allowing you to keep your property
- applies the rules to common types of assets
- discusses the degree to which the law permits you to convert nonexempt assets into exempt assets on the eve of bankruptcy.

It's essential to keep in mind that even if the bankruptcy trustee can't take it, a creditor with a security interest in an asset may be able to cause you grief. This topic is discussed generally in chapter 6, "Don't Lien on Me." It is also addressed in chapter 8, "Cars and Household Goods," and in chapter 9, "Home Sweet Home."

65

LEGAL HOKEYPOKEY

Determining which assets are included in your bankruptcy is a little like doing the hokeypokey. One law puts an item into your bankruptcy; another law allows you to take it back out.

The Bankruptcy Code says all the assets you own on the petition date are property of the estate, which means that the property is subject to the bankruptcy. But other laws provide for exemptions, which allow you to pull the property out of the bankruptcy.

In most situations, the rules on whether an item is property of the estate are the same, no matter where you file bankruptcy. But the types of property you may pull out of your bankruptcy under exemption laws depend on where you live when you file. Each state seems to have a different idea of what property should be exempt, and some of those ideas are rather bizarre.

• In Pennsylvania an unmarried debtor may exempt only a few items of personal property, whereas a debtor in Florida can exempt a homestead of $1 million!

• Rhode Island exempts dead bodies. Yes, dead bodies. Go figure.

• Puerto Rican miners can exempt their home, so long as it's not worth more than $200. Apparently, mining isn't terribly profitable in Puerto Rico.

• Also in Puerto Rico, doctors can exempt their horse and carriage, so long as they use them for house calls.

Your exemptions are determined by the law of the state where you lived for the longest portion of the 180-day period immediately preceding the petition date. (Appendix 3 provides a rundown of the various state exemption laws.) Some people have even moved to a different state to take advantage of that state's more liberal exemption policy. But the courts have recently been adopting rules to discourage this practice.

Property of the Estate

Property of the estate includes all the assets you own on the petition date, plus inheritances, life insurance, and divorce property settlements to which you become entitled within 180 days after that point.

If someone owes you money on the date you file bankruptcy, that asset is property of the estate, even though it is not paid until later. A common example is your income tax refund, which is property of the estate even if not paid until after the petition date.

In 1985 a debtor won $3 million in the Connecticut State Lottery, payable in annual installments of $128,000. During the next six years, creditors lent him so much money that he had to file bankruptcy. The court declared the balance of his winnings was property of the estate.

Likewise, accrued wages are also included in the estate, even though you don't receive them until after the petition date. Reason: they were actually earned before you filed. It sounds confusing, but it's really not that difficult.

Let's say you've got a job where you get paid weekly. Usually, your paycheck covers the previous week, not the current one, so the employer is always a week behind. So if you filed bankruptcy on the day after payday, your employer would owe you one week's pay as of that date. For bankruptcy purposes, the wages you have earned become property of the estate, even if you haven't yet received them.

But don't sweat it too much. Most, if not all, of that money will ultimately be exempt anyhow.

Of course, an asset owned by someone else doesn't become part of your bankruptcy just because you may have physical control of it. For example, the lawn mower you borrowed from your neighbor is not included in your bankruptcy just because you keep it in your garage.

Or if, for convenience, you are an authorized signer on your elderly aunt's bank account, the account does not become part of your bankruptcy if all the money really belongs to her.

Similarly, property belonging to your children is not included in your bankruptcy. But don't try to protect your property by signing it over to your kids, or you'll probably get nailed for a *fraudulent transfer* (see discussion in chapter 7, "Games People Play").

Exemptions

Although bankruptcy law is generally the province of the feds, some jurisdictions have their own provisions with regard to exemptions, giving people the chance to pick and choose between exemptions offered under the U.S. Bankruptcy Code and those provided by their own legislature.

For instance, in the following jurisdictions debtors can select exemptions under the Bankruptcy Code or local exemptions: Alaska, Arkansas, Connecticut, District of Columbia, Hawaii, Massachusetts, Michigan, Minnesota, New Jersey, New Mexico, Pennsylvania, Puerto Rico, Rhode Island, South Carolina, Texas, Vermont, Virgin Islands, Washington, and Wisconsin.

Even in states where you can choose between state and Bankruptcy Code exemptions, you have to take the whole set; you can't pick and choose between them. Also, joint debtors must both agree to choose state exemptions. In other words, one spouse can't pluck the state exemptions if the other elects to go the federal route.

There are some federal exemptions in statutes other than the Bankruptcy Code, and these can be claimed in all states. They include:

- veterans' benefits and military pensions
- railroad retirement payments
- social security benefits
- longshoremen's and harbor workers' death and disability benefits
- seamen's wages
- special pensions awarded to Congressional Medal of Honor winners.

The Bankruptcy Code, like state laws, comes with a smorgasbord of exemptions, including: personal injury claims and workers' compensation claims, support payments due to a debtor, and interests in certain types of insurance policies.

But the amount of the exemption and the types of property to which it applies vary widely from state to state. For example, common items such as firearms, cameras, and golf clubs are considered household goods in some states but not in others.

Why It Matters

The principles behind property of the estate and exemptions are important in both Chapter 7 and Chapter 13 cases.

In a Chapter 7 you lose any asset that is property of the estate unless it is exempt. In a Chapter 13 your minimum payments are determined by the value of your nonexempt property. For example, if the value of your nonexempt property is $7,500, you would have to pay at least that much over the life of your Chapter 13 plan.

In summary, the first issue is whether an asset is property of the estate. If it is, don't despair because it still might be exempt. If property is exempt, you still get to keep it in a Chapter 7 and it won't affect the payment amount in a Chapter 13.

COMMON TYPES OF PROPERTY

There are special rules about how certain property is treated in bankruptcy. The most common are discussed in this section.

Homesteads

Almost all states have some type of homestead exemption protecting some or all of the equity in a debtor's home.

Equity is determined by establishing the value of your home (a good place to start is the local real property tax assessor's office) and subtracting your mortgage and other secured loans. If your home is worth $150,000 and you owe $100,000 against it, your equity is $50,000.

Preserving your homestead is not always a simple matter, and you could unwittingly lose your exemption. Some states require that you actually live in the home, whereas others permit temporary absences or require only that a family member live there.

If you are considering bankruptcy, consult a bankruptcy lawyer before refinancing your home, renting it out, moving, signing a contract to sell, making improvements, or allowing a judgment or tax lien to be filed. While a Chapter 13 is open, it is very risky to rent out, move, or enter into a contract to sell your homestead without first checking with your lawyer.

Homestead exemptions are discussed in more detail in chapter 9, "Home Sweet Home," and in appendix 3.

After Andy was convicted of selling a few joints from his home, the state started a forfeiture proceeding to take his home under drug laws that allow seizure of property used in the sale of illegal drugs. He thought that Chapter 13 might protect his home. No luck. The court said that neither the automatic stay nor homestead exemptions apply in drug forfeiture proceedings.

Automobiles

Most states allow debtors to exempt at least one motor vehicle, but they limit the amount of the exemption. If your equity in a car exceeds the exemption, a Chapter 7 trustee could sell the car and pay you the value of your exemption.

For example, if your state allows a $1,500 exemption for an automobile and yours is worth $2,500, the trustee could sell your car but would have to pay you $1,500.

In a Chapter 13 the trustee could not sell the car, but you would have to pay the amount of nonexempt equity, $1,000, over the life of the plan.

Automobile exemptions are discussed in more detail in chapter 8, "Cars and Household Goods," and in appendix 3.

Household Goods

Ordinary household goods are almost entirely exempt. Again, these exemptions are discussed in more detail in chapter 8 and appendix 3.

Inheritances and Life Insurance Benefits

If you become entitled to these benefits within 180 days of filing, they will be applied to payment of your debts. You are considered entitled to an inheritance or life insurance proceeds when the person dies, even though the money is to be paid much later.

If your benefactor has already died before you file bankruptcy, there may be a way to prevent your inheritance from going to the trustee.

Thelma's grandfather, who had bequeathed his Aspen ski chalet to Thelma, suffered a stroke the day before her 341 meeting. Her grandfather survived, and her eventual inheritance was safe. If he died within 180 days of the petition date, the chalet would have been sold to pay creditors.

In some states you can "renounce" an inheritance before you actually receive it, and the property will go to one of the other heirs. This strategy is very tricky, and there are many pitfalls, but it's something to bring up with your lawyer.

Divorce Settlements

Many times, divorce and bankruptcy go hand in hand. If you are in the midst of a divorce, remember that if, within 180 days after your petition date, you become entitled to a divorce property settlement, the property could be used to pay creditors.

Gretchen filed for divorce and bankruptcy on the same day. Four months later, the divorce court awarded Gretchen all of her husband's IBM stock as a property settlement. To Gretchen's dismay, the bankruptcy trustee then seized the stock, sold it, and used the proceeds to pay creditors.

Sometimes it's better to file bankruptcy and wait 180 days before filing for divorce. And of course, make sure that your divorce lawyer knows about your bankruptcy plans, and your bankruptcy lawyer knows about your divorce.

Spendthrift Trusts

Oftentimes, a wise benefactor will shield assets of a young or seemingly reckless beneficiary through what is called a *spendthrift trust*. Here's how it works: someone wills or gives you a sum of money but appoints a trustee to dole out the funds and specifies that the inheritance or gift can't be touched by your creditors while in the custody of the trustee.

The logic behind this apparent loophole is twofold. First, your creditors are not harmed by this restriction because they never could have relied on someone's making you a gift. Second, except for your "allowance," even you couldn't force the trustee to give you the money, so your creditors shouldn't be able to do so either.

Therefore, if someone sets up a trust for you and provides that it is not subject to claims of your creditors, the Bankruptcy Code and the courts hold that this property interest does not become property of the estate.

But there are a number of commonsensical restrictions. For example:

• You can't place your own property in "trust" for yourself and hope to keep it away from your creditors. There are some self-anointed experts who, touting "living trusts," might tell you differently. Don't believe them.

• You can't be the sole trustee and sole beneficiary of the trust at the same time, even if it is set up by someone else. The courts are not going to allow you to shield money if you have sole discretion over how and when it is distributed.

The most important thing to remember about trusts is that the rules are technical and extremely tricky. Your lawyer should review all trust documents to determine whether you are risking your interest in the trust by filing bankruptcy.

Rent Receipts

Be careful if you are renting out any property to others. Any income earned by property of the estate is itself property of the estate. The trustee may have a claim to any rents received from your property after the petition date.

In many cases debtors are allowed to use rent receipts to make their postpetition mortgage payments on the property. However, you should get the trustee's consent first. Otherwise, he or she may insist that you reimburse the estate for any rents collected after the petition date. Just imagine the predicament you'd be in if you had already spent the money.

Wages

As we said, wages that you have earned as of the petition date are property of the estate even though they are not paid until afterward. Nevertheless, a large portion is exempt.

You can minimize the wages that are at risk by filing your petition soon after your payday. (Of course, you will want to spend this money before filing because the funds on hand on the petition date would also be property of the estate.)

> A professional football player filed bankruptcy in the middle of the season. His salary for playing sixteen games was $575,000 payable in weekly installments of $35,937.50. The court held that pay for the seven games played before the petition date was property of the estate, but the money he earned for the remaining nine games was his.

Commissions

If you work on commission, any commissions you earned before filing are property of the estate.

Commissions are a little tricky when it comes to insurance agents, who usually get an automatic cut every time a customer renews a policy. The issue of *renewal commissions* is somewhat unsettled.

Trustees frequently try to latch on to all future renewal commissions from any policy initially sold before the petition date. Their argument is based on the premise that all the work was done when the policy was sold, so they are like accounts receivable owed on the petition date. Insurance agents counter that policyholders won't renew unless the agent continues to keep in contact with, and service, the account. Therefore renewal commissions, in the view of insurance agents, are attributable to postpetition services and not property of the estate.

Some courts buy the trustee's argument. Some go with the insurance agent's. Others take a middle road by figuring out how much of a commission is attributable to prepetition work, and how much is due to postpetition efforts. Only that portion of the commission resulting from prepetition efforts is property of the estate. The rest goes to the debtor.

In some states, commissions are considered wages, so a large portion might still be exempt.

Severance Pay

Watch out if your job entitles you to severance pay. The trustee can't force you to quit your job, of course. But if you do terminate your employment while the bankruptcy case is still open, the trustee might claim these benefits, arguing that they actually are compensation for prebankruptcy services.

Suits to Recover Money

A suit to recover money is property of the estate, even though you do not expect to receive any money until later.

Luckily, however, there is an exemption for part or all of personal injury awards, depending on whether the award is for past earnings, medical bills, pain and suffering, or future earnings.

If possible, settle the claim before bankruptcy because your attorney can structure the settlement to maximize the amount that is exempt. For example, many exemption statutes say that personal injury awards for lost earnings are exempt while those for pain and suffering are not. Your lawyer could devise a settlement agreement where most of the award is allocated to items that would normally be exempt. Be sure to tell your personal injury lawyer that you are thinking about bankruptcy, and insist that she or he have a bankruptcy specialist review any settlement documents before they are signed.

Any funds received from the settlement should be placed in a separate bank account so that they can be identified as the proceeds of your personal injury claim.

If the claim cannot be settled before bankruptcy, the trustee can take over the prosecution of the suit and control the structure of the settlement so as to maximize the part that is not exempt. In this situation you should consider a Chapter 13 instead of Chapter 7 because most courts allow you to control the structure of the settlement.

But watch out! A few courts have gone off the deep end and held that all the proceeds of a personal injury lawsuit must be used to pay creditors, even the part that should be exempt. Let's hope that Congress or the appellate courts will straighten this out, but in any event your lawyer should know what position your local bankruptcy court takes on this question.

Income Tax Refunds

Similarly, an income tax refund for the year the bankruptcy was filed and any tax year ending before that is property of the estate, even though you don't receive the money until after the petition date.

One way to avoid this outcome is to have a tax preparation company that offers "rapid refunds" prepare your return. This way you can get at least the federal refund immediately and spend it on food, rent, and other living expenses before you file.

Unfortunately, things are not so simple if you owe the government money. The IRS has the right to deduct any taxes you owe from your refund, and several federal statutes give other government agencies this right as well. If you owe guaranteed student loans, the government will try to take your refund.

In some situations your refund can be diverted to satisfy past-due support obligations if public assistance was paid to either your ex-spouse or your child. Also, your refunds for years after the petition date might be in jeopardy, unless the tax, student loan, or other government debt is discharged.

Pensions

Pensions are complicated. But it's safe to say that if your pension is covered by a federal law entitled the Employee Retirement Income Security Act of 1974 (ERISA), it is protected.

Most private pensions are covered by ERISA, and they are protected even if there is no exemption because they do not become property of the estate.

If your retirement plan is not covered by ERISA—as is the case with government pensions, pensions that primarily benefit only the owners of the business, and private plans such as IRAs—then the plan is property of the estate and is protected only to the extent that there is an applicable federal or state exemption.

If there is no exemption for IRAs in your state, these plans are not protected, even though the IRS can impose a tax penalty for withdrawing the money prior to retirement. Fortunately, IRAs are covered by exemptions in most states.

Chances are pretty good that your retirement plan will not be affected by your bankruptcy. (However, as noted earlier, you probably won't be allowed to contribute to your retirement or 401K plan.) But the story could be different if you made any unusual contributions to your pension, such as taking a large sum of nonexempt cash and depositing it in your pension account. Also, courts will not let you get away with borrowing money and socking it into an exempt pension.

EXEMPTION PLANNING

To a limited degree, the law allows some prebankruptcy planning to maximize exemptions. For example: If you had $1,000 in a bank account on the petition date, it would not be exempt. But if you took that $1,000 and made extra payments on your mortgage before filing bankruptcy, the increase in equity in your homestead might be exempt.

CAUTION! Exemption planning is an extremely complicated and unsettled area of the law. If you go too far, there are serious consequences. Consult a bankruptcy attorney *before* engaging in any prebankruptcy planning.

CAUTION! There is a big difference between converting your property into exempt assets that you continue to own and placing property in someone else's name.

Transferring property to someone else is considered fraudulent if the court thinks you did it to keep assets out of reach of creditors. Don't make any gifts or sell any property for less than it's worth before filing bankruptcy. If you have already done so, be sure to tell your bankruptcy lawyer.

> It was a close call, but the bankruptcy court sided with Lance. The judge was convinced that Lance planned to retire in Florida *before* he ran into financial trouble. Otherwise, the court might well have forced Lance to sell his new home to pay off creditors. Lance escaped financial ruin by the skin of his teeth.

6

DON'T LIEN ON ME

As a poor kid growing up in a shack, Gloria dreamed of the day when she'd have her own apartment, with real furniture rather than makeshift chairs pieced together from pilfered cinder blocks and scrap wood. So after earning her degree and landing a good job at a brokerage firm, Gloria used her newly acquired credit to furnish her new apartment. When the firm suddenly disbanded and Gloria lost her job, she had to file bankruptcy and feared losing her cherished furniture. But all Gloria had to give up was the end table she had bought on a department store charge account.

There always seems to be a catch-22 in the law, and that's especially true in bankruptcy. Although a lot of your assets might be exempt (see the section on exemptions in chapter 5, "What Do You Have to Lose?") in a bankruptcy proceeding, you're still not quite as safe as you might think. A *lien*, which is simply a legal claim on your property as security for a debt, can complicate things and cause you all kinds of grief. But there are steps you can, and should, take to protect yourself. Just knowing the score puts you ahead in this game.

With even a basic understanding of some elementary legal principles, you will be in a much better position to protect, to whatever extent the law will allow, your home, car, and other possessions.

This chapter explains:

- the legal meaning of *property ownership*
- the nature of a lien, as a form of ownership
- the difference between consensual and nonconsensual liens

- how a lien is "perfected"
- how liens are handled in bankruptcy.

It also illustrates that there are three people who might have an interest in one or more of your assets: you, the trustee, and a secured creditor.

PROPERTY OWNERSHIP: A "BUNDLE OF RIGHTS"

Ownership and property are really two sides of the same coin because the law defines property as that bundle of ownership rights in an asset which our society recognizes and protects.

This bundle of rights can be divvied up among several people, so that each has some ownership rights at the same time.

Sole Ownership

If you own an asset "free and clear," you hold the entire bundle of the rights associated with it. No one else shares in those rights.

Let's say you purchased a television with cash; then you alone have all the ownership rights that go along with it. When your car is paid off, the result is the same.

This bundle of rights includes the right to possession and the right to sell the item and keep all the money.

Joint Ownership

Two people can share ownership of an asset at the same time.

For example, if you and your spouse bought your home together, each of you would have a right to possession and neither could sell it without the other's consent. In addition, the proceeds from the sale of the asset would rightfully be divided between you.

Ownership and Possession

You've heard it said that possession is nine-tenths of the law. It's not quite that simple. The bundle of rights can be divided up in many different ways.

You could, for example, transfer only your right to possession but retain the right to sell the asset and keep the proceeds. A perfect example is a leased apartment. When you lease an apartment, the landlord retains all the elements of ownership except the right of possession, which he or she transfers to you. So long as the rent is paid, the landlord is not entitled to possession; you are.

Property as Collateral

Another way to divide the bundle of rights is to pledge an asset as collateral for a debt. In that case, you and the creditor share the ownership rights connected with the asset.

While you may retain the right to possession, the creditor may have the right to prevent you from selling the asset without its consent, plus the right to some of the proceeds if you do sell it. And your ownership becomes conditional: if the obligation is not satisfied, the creditor gets the asset.

The most important point is this: you could lose property that might normally be shielded in bankruptcy, if it has a lien on it.

THE LOWDOWN ON LIENS

The term *lien* describes a category of property interests in an asset that secures the payment of some obligation. When there is a lien against property, the property is said to be *encumbered* by the lien.

Liens can be divided into two types: *consensual liens* and *nonconsensual liens*.

Consensual Liens

These are liens that you voluntarily grant to someone else. Consensual liens on personal property are called *security interests*.

Example: When you signed your home mortgage, you voluntarily granted the bank a lien in the form of a mortgage and thereby transferred some of your ownership rights to the bank. You retained the right of possession and gave the bank the right to some of the proceeds if you sold the property.

In giving a mortgage, you also made your ownership conditional. In other words, the bank agreed to lend you money, and you agreed that the bank could take possession and sell the property if you didn't pay back the loan. So under the law, both you and the bank simultaneously have ownership interests, albeit different ownership interests. Similarly, if you grant a lender a lien on your car, you give up some of your ownership rights.

Loans from consumer finance companies often carry a security interest in your household goods. In theory, this gives the loan company the right to seize and sell all your earthly belongings. But it's not really as bad as it sounds. We'll discuss this topic in more detail in chapter 7, "Games People Play."

There are a couple of other terms and concepts that apply here:

- *Purchase money security interests,* where the proceeds of the loan are used to purchase a specific item.
- *Nonpurchase money security interests,* which attach to property you already own.

When you charge items at some department stores, the papers you sign give them a purchase money security interest in the property you buy. So if a department store lends you money to buy a microwave oven, for example, it reserves the right to take back the appliance if you don't pay. But such security interests are fairly rare. Usually, when you buy something on credit, there is no security interest, so even though you fail to pay the bill the creditor can't repossess whatever it was that you bought.

Nonconsensual Liens

Sometimes the law gives creditors a lien on your property without your consent, and these are called nonconsensual liens.

For example, real property taxes are liens against your property even though you never directly consent (although it could be argued, perhaps, that merely purchasing property subject to taxation would constitute implicit consent). The same holds true with a judgment lien. When a judgment is entered against you in some courts, it becomes a lien against your real property, which secures payment of the judgment.

The key point to remember is that nonconsensual liens are actual ownership interests in your property, just like consensual liens. But since you never specifically agreed to these liens, the Bankruptcy Code gives them less protection than it gives to consensual liens. In chapter 7, "Games People Play," we'll discuss in more detail how some nonconsensual liens can be avoided.

How a Lien Is Enforced

When someone has a lien on your property, the law usually requires the lien holder to take certain steps to warn others that he or she has some of the ownership rights associated with the collateral. When these steps have been taken, the lien is considered "perfected." Usually, some sort of public recording is required.

For example, your home mortgage is not perfected until the mortgage document is recorded in the county real property records. Also, in most states a security interest in a motor vehicle is not perfected until the creditor is listed as a lien holder on the certificate of title.

Perfection is an important concept to understand because, as we discuss in chapter 7, "Games People Play," the trustee has the power to avoid unperfected liens and take over that creditor's ownership rights.

Treatment of Liens in Bankruptcy

As we have seen, someone with a lien on one of your assets has an actual ownership interest, separate from your interests and those of the trustee. The practical application of that principle is as follows:

Let's say your home is worth $75,000, you owe the bank $25,000 on your mortgage, and state law gives you an exemption of $20,000. If you declare bankruptcy, the bank has an ownership interest in the property up to the amount of the loan, or $25,000 in this case. You have an interest equal to your $20,000 exemption, and the trustee has an ownership interest in the nonexempt equity of $30,000.

We have already seen that the automatic stay that goes into effect when a bankruptcy petition is filed prevents repossession or foreclosure without the court's consent. And as we will see in the next chapter, debtors and trustees have the power to avoid some liens. We'll also see how a debtor can restructure the obligations and redeem the property from the liens.

> Gloria was able to keep most of her furniture because there were no liens and she hadn't, in a legal sense, shared her ownership rights. She lost the end table, however, because in the fine print on the department store charge account there was a lien provision.

7

. . . .

GAMES PEOPLE PLAY

Joan thought she was being clever. She transferred her vacation home to her daughter, didn't bother telling her lawyer about the transaction, and conveniently neglected to mention it in her bankruptcy papers. Who would ever know? Anyone who wants to, that's who.

Bankruptcy fraud is, plain and simply, stupid, and the chances of getting caught are increasing all the time.

A special task force including the FBI, the IRS, U.S. attorney's office, the U.S. Postal Service, and the U.S. trustee's office was assembled in 1994 to track down cheats. Additionally, the FBI is sponsoring training sessions to help lawyers and paralegals spot fraud. Nationally, there were 106 convictions for bankruptcy fraud in 1993, a 49 percent increase from the year before.

Obviously, authorities are taking a closer look at bankruptcy cases and are growing leery of debtors who try to stiff creditors—and hide behind the shield of the court—by playing games like transferring assets and commingling business and personal funds.

Don't even think about using such tactics. As noted earlier, debtors' prisons are a thing of the past. But there is plenty of room in the federal penitentiaries for debtors who try to manipulate the system.

Even if you don't end up in prison, playing games can have serious consequences. This chapter addresses:

- the trustee's power to avoid fraudulent transfers
- the trustee's power to avoid preferential transfers

- the relationship between preferential transfers and avoidable liens
- the debtor's power to avoid judgment liens
- the debtor's power to avoid security interests
- the power of Chapter 13 debtors to modify liens and restructure obligations
- the power of Chapter 7 debtors to redeem personal property from a lien.

AN ADVERSARIAL PROCESS

Bankruptcy, like the American judicial system in general, is an adversarial process. In theory, justice results when parties with conflicting interests compete against each other under an established set of rules. The courtroom is the playing field, and the judge is the referee.

With that as its guiding principle, the Bankruptcy Code seeks to achieve a fair distribution of assets to creditors while still allowing debtors to keep the property needed for a fresh start.

The law gives creditors, trustees, and debtors weapons and expects them to fight it out. These weapons include *avoidance powers*, which allow the trustee and debtor to avoid certain liens and transfers of property.

If you don't know about these avoidance powers, you may be in for unpleasant surprises in your bankruptcy and might not take advantage of all the benefits bankruptcy offers.

THE TRUSTEE'S AVOIDANCE POWERS

The trustee's avoidance powers are designed to help him or her recover assets and distribute the proceeds fairly to unsecured creditors. Although Chapter 7 and Chapter 13 trustees have the same avoidance powers, they are most commonly employed in Chapter 7.

The trustee has the power to "avoid" or undo: fraudulent transfers, preferential transfers, and unperfected liens. Let's discuss each of these powers in turn.

Fraudulent Transfers

The trustee can "avoid" any prepetition transfer that is considered fraudulent. Transfers of this type are usually misguided attempts by people with debt problems to put property in someone else's name and to keep their stuff at arm's length from creditors. This is considered cheating, and there are serious consequences.

Celeste talked her way into a sixty-day jail term and four months of home detention after lying to the bankruptcy court and fraudulently concealing assets—namely, artwork, furniture, and money she was making on the sly through her under-the-table escort service. Celeste now has a criminal record, and she owes $25,000 restitution to her creditors.

Common examples of fraudulent transfers include:

- placing title to a car in a friend's name with the secret understanding that it will be transferred back some day
- "selling" property for much less than it's worth, with the understanding that you can later "buy" it back
- making a gift of property to a friend or relative to prevent a creditor from getting it.

Fraudulent Transfers Among Friends and Lovers. When two people live together, but only one files bankruptcy, there are many possibilities for fraudulent transfers, and the trustee will be inclined to examine the situation carefully.

If you used your money to contribute to the purchase of household goods or a car used by both you and your roommate, you won't get away with claiming that your roomie is the sole owner of the property. Similarly, there is a possibility that the court would find fraud if you claimed that all your contributions to the household went for living expenses and all property was purchased and owned by your roommate.

Joint bank accounts can be a problem. If you maintained a joint account with your roommate and tried to claim that all your money was spent on living expenses and any balance belongs to your room-mate, the court would likely be skeptical.

Shortly before filing bankruptcy, a debtor paid $100,000 to attend a fund-raising dinner with then President George Bush. But the court made the Republican National Committee turn the money over to a trustee. Reason: the court deemed the conveyance invalid on the theory that the contributor got "less than reasonably equivalent value" for the investment.

Preferential Transfers

The other common avoidance power of the trustee has nothing to do with bad conduct. Rather, it is just designed to implement what Congress thought was a fair way to distribute assets. This is the power to avoid preferential transfers.

Congress considers it unfair for one unsecured creditor to get a payment on the eve of bankruptcy when others are left holding the bag. So it gave the trustee the power to recover these payments for the benefit of all unsecured creditors.

For example, if a month before bankruptcy you paid your dentist $1,000 on an overdue bill, the trustee could get this money back from the dentist and distribute it to all your unsecured creditors. The end result would be that you wasted the $1,000. And it would be even worse if you paid that money toward a nondischargeable debt. In that case, if the trustee "avoided" the payment, you would have wasted the money—and the amount of the nondischargeable debt would increase by the amount recovered by the trustee.

How Preferential Transfers Differ from Fraudulent Transfers. Fraudulent transfers are cheating; preferential transfers are not. So long as there is a legitimate debt that is paid, the transfer might be preferential, but it is not fraudulent. The distinction is very important because your discharge can be denied for making a fraudulent transfer but not for a preferential transfer.

Time Limitations on Preferences. Preferential transfers can be recovered only if made within a specified time before bankruptcy, usually ninety days.

Incidentally, if you make a payment by check, the key date is when the check actually clears, not when you deliver it.

But watch out for payments to *insiders*, even if the debt is legitimate. Here the time period is a whole year. The trustee may be able to recover all the payments made to an insider during the entire year before bankruptcy (see section below on cosigned loans).

Insiders include relatives and others with a close enough relationship with you to strongly influence your actions. If you are still friends with your ex-spouse, he or she might be considered an insider; if you're bitter enemies, probably not. A live-in lover would probably be considered an insider. Whether an individual qualifies as an insider is determined on a case-by-case basis.

Payments That Are Not Preferences. The following types of payments are not preferences because of special exceptions in the Bankruptcy Code:

- *Small payments.* If payments to any single creditor during the relevant time period total less than $600, they are not avoidable.
- *Payments on secured debts.* Payments on your house or car, for example, are not recoverable as preferences. You can and should continue making these payments if you intend to keep your house or vehicle.
- *Payments for current expenses.* Regular payments on bills that are not overdue are not avoidable. For example, your rent payment for the current month would not be avoidable, but if you paid back rent totaling more than $600, it would be.
- *Payments of back alimony or child support.* Under the 1994 amendments, payments to an ex-spouse for back alimony or child support cannot be recovered by the trustee.

Cosigned Loans. If you possess cosigned or guaranteed loans, be careful.

Let's say your Uncle Joe cosigned so you could get an unsecured bank loan. In effect, he promised the bank that if you couldn't pay, he would. Since every payment you make to the bank also reduces the amount of your uncle's potential liability, the law treats any payment you make to the bank as also a payment to your uncle—even though your uncle doesn't actually receive any money!

And let's say that you got behind in the payments over the last year but, to protect your uncle, managed to pay the bank $1,500. The trustee could recover this money from your uncle even though he never got a cent.

Remember that the relevant time period for payments benefiting an insider is a whole year. If your cosigner is an insider, the trustee can recover all payments made on the cosigned loan within the past year.

On the other hand, if a casual friend, rather than an insider, cosigned, the trustee could recover only payments made during the ninety days before the petition date.

Many people try to protect cosigners by paying the debt before filing bankruptcy. As you can see, that's a mistake. Instead of making payments yourself, it would be much better to explain things to the cosigner and have him or her make the payments until after you file bankruptcy. You can always reimburse the cosigner later.

Unperfected Liens

The law requires lien holders to "perfect" their liens to warn people that someone other than you claims an interest in your property. For example, mortgages must be recorded, and security interests in motor vehicles must be noted on the certificate of title.

If the lien holder has not perfected a lien by the time a bankruptcy petition is filed, it's too late and the trustee could take over the creditor's interest in the asset.

For example, assume that you owed the bank $4,000 on a car with a book value of $5,000 and that the exemption amount is $1,500. Usually, your exemption would cover any equity in the car, the bank would have its security interest, and there would be nothing for the trustee. If you wanted to keep the car, you would continue to make the payments to the bank.

But if it turned out that the bank, when it loaned you the money, forgot to have its lien on your car noted on the certificate of title, the trustee could take over the bank's security interest. If this happened, you would have to make payments not to the bank but to the trustee.

More important, as discussed below, if the trustee avoids the security interest, any prepetition payments on the loan become vulnerable to preference attack, with some surprising consequences.

Unperfection and Preferences

When the trustee avoids a lien because it's unperfected, new preference issues crop up.

Remember that payments on secured loans are not avoidable preferences, but payments on unsecured loans may be? Well, if the trustee avoids a lien, the loan is considered to have been unsecured all the time, so all prepetition payments to the creditor within the relevant time period become avoidable preferences.

For example, assume your uncle cosigned on your secured car loan and during the past year you paid $1,500 on the loan. Ordinarily, these payments would not be avoidable preferences because they were made to a secured creditor.

But let's say the bank forgot to have its security interest noted on the certificate of title and the trustee avoided it. In that situation all the loan payments become preferences, and the trustee could recover this money from your uncle. Further, since you would be making future payments to the trustee, rather than the bank, your uncle would still have to pay the bank. The bottom line is that your uncle would remain on the hook, even though the bank lost its security interest to the trustee.

Another wrinkle: We know that the trustee can recover payments and other transfers of property on old debts made during the preference period. Well, the act of perfecting a lien is considered to be a transfer of property, so if a lien is not perfected at the same time that the loan is made, attempted perfection later would be an avoidable preference if done during the preference period.

Example: The bank that made your car loan discovered that it had failed to have its security interest noted on the certificate of title when it made the loan. It might try to "fix" the error later by having its security interest added to the certificate of title. This attempt would be an avoidable transfer if done within the preference period.

Key Points

Obviously, the law is pretty complicated on the subject of preferences. Here, in a nutshell, are the key points that you should remember:

- Before the first meeting with your bankruptcy attorney, get copies of your loan documents and bring them with you so that the lawyer can determine if there are any problems. For your mortgage you'll need copies of the mortgage document itself showing the recorder's stamp and the date of recording. For your car you'll need a copy of the certificate of title. The lender should give you these for the asking.
- After you decide to file bankruptcy, don't make payments on old unsecured debts—unless the debt is less than $600 and you don't want to include it in your bankruptcy.
- If you have a cosigned debt and are worried that the creditor will come after the cosigner if you miss payments, have the cosigner make payments until after your bankruptcy is filed.
- Be sure to tell your lawyer about all preferential payments you've made.
- If you owe money to a friend or relative, you can pay him or her after bankruptcy but not before.
- Payments on your mortgage or car are not avoidable preferences because they are probably secured debts. But your lawyer should look at the loan documents to make sure the creditor did the paperwork right and the debt is really secured.
- Courts differ on whether tax payments are avoidable preferences, so check with your lawyer before paying taxes. You should also check with your lawyer to see if there is any advantage to your specifying the taxes to which any payments should be applied.
- Borrowing money from one creditor to pay another on the eve of bankruptcy might be considered fraudulent as to the first creditor, and if so, the debt would not be discharged.
- Loans to pay federal income taxes are not discharged.

YOUR AVOIDANCE POWERS AND OTHER WEAPONS

The trustee is not the only one with avoidance powers. The Bankruptcy Code gives debtors the power to avoid some kinds of liens that interfere with their exemptions.

Security Interests in Household Goods and Tools

Consumer loan companies frequently take a security interest in all your earthly belongings when you borrow money from them. This means that the loan company—unless you file bankruptcy—can take your stuff if you don't pay the loan. The Bankruptcy Code gives you the power to avoid these security interests, keep the property, and wipe out the debt at the same time.

But this avoidance power does not apply to purchase money security interests. As we explained in chapter 6, "Don't Lien on Me," when you borrow money to buy a specific item and give a security interest to secure payment, this is a purchase money security interest.

For example, if you bought a television on a charge account, the fine print gives the department store a security interest in the TV. You could not avoid this security interest (although you could redeem, reaffirm, or, in Chapter 13, "cramdown" the debt).

Tools to a mechanic are like ice cream to a kid. Every time the Acme Tool truck showed up at Mort's shop, he bought some gadget and added it to his account. When he filed bankruptcy, Acme pulled out the papers that Mort signed when he opened his account and claimed a purchase money security interest in all the tools Mort had ever bought, insisting that he either give them back, pay their value, or reaffirm the debt. But the court said Mort could keep the tools without paying for them because Acme couldn't prove how it allocated the payments Mort had made on the account.

But there's a twist. As you make more purchases from the same store, the purchases are added to your account and you make a single monthly payment on all your purchases. How can anyone tell if a specific item is paid off? For example, assume that you make the following purchases from a department store: a TV in February, a washer in April, and a bed in December. Then you also make some payments on the account that total the price of the first purchase.

The courts say that, in this situation, the creditor has to prove that it allocated payments to specific purchases. If it can't, then no part of the security interest qualifies for "purchase money" status, which means you can avoid the security interest to the extent that the purchases would otherwise be exempt. In the above example, if the store can't prove how each payment was allocated, you can avoid the security interest in all the items.

Judgment Liens

A judgment lien is a nonconsensual lien, for the simple reason that it is imposed against your property without your consent. When a judgment is entered against you in some courts, it automatically becomes a lien on all your real property.

To illustrate this idea, let's say your home is worth $75,000 and is subject to a mortgage lien of $55,000. Assume further that you owe $15,000 in medical bills. If the equity in your home is $20,000 and your state permits a homestead exemption of $20,000, you could file bankruptcy, discharge the medical bills, and keep your home by continuing to pay the mortgage. However, let's say the hospital sued you before you filed bankruptcy and got a judgment lien for $15,000. That lien would devour all but $5,000 of your homestead exemption, and after the bankruptcy you would still have to pay both your mortgage and the judgment if you wanted to keep your home.

Congress didn't think this was fair, so it put a section in the Bankruptcy Code allowing debtors to avoid such a judgment to the extent that it impairs a homestead exemption . . . as of the petition date. But the code did not address the situation where the property appreciates after that.

For example, let's say that on the petition date your home is worth $75,000, you owe $50,000 on your mortgage, and there is a judgment lien against the property securing a $12,000 judgment. Assume that your state allows a homestead exemption up to $30,000. Your equity on the petition date after deducting your mortgage is $25,000 ($75,000 – $50,000). Since the equity is within your $30,000 exemption, the judgment lien can be "avoided." But what happens down the road, when the property has appreciated and is now worth $100,000 and you have reduced your mortgage to $35,000? Your equity after deducting the mortgage is $65,000 ($100,000 − $35,000). Now that your equity exceeds your $30,000 homestead exemption, does the judgment lien that was "avoided" in your bankruptcy spring back and reattach to your home?

Quite a few courts said that it does.

Many people thought that the reattachment of a judgment lien interfered with debtors' "fresh start" because a large portion of the mortgage payments debtors made after bankruptcy went to benefit the holder of the lien.

In the 1994 amendments, Congress intended to fix this problem, so that once a judgment lien is avoided in bankruptcy, it's gone forever and doesn't reattach later. Unfortunately, the language Congress used is not very clear on this point, and the courts will have to decide whether Congress actually accomplished its objective.

Rather than relying on ongoing legal interpretations, you are much better off filing bankruptcy before the lien is imposed.

If a judgment lien has already attached to your homestead, you could sell your home immediately after the bankruptcy and buy a new one. In that case the judgment lien would not attach to your new home because the debt was discharged and any increase in value would be all yours.

The 1994 amendments also give special protection to judgments entered by divorce courts for alimony and child support, but it's not clear whether a divorce judgment securing a property division would also be protected.

Redemption

In addition to the avoidance powers discussed above, a Chapter 7 debtor has the right to "redeem" consumer goods by paying the creditor not the amount of the debt but a lump sum equal to its value. With personal property, this is almost always less than the amount of the debt. The problem is that unless the creditor agrees otherwise, this payment must be made in a lump sum and within about forty days after the petition date.

Additional Powers of a Chapter 13 Debtor

In Chapter 13, a debtor can modify liens and restructure loans as in the following example: If your car is worth $4,000 and you owe $5,000, you could pay the value of the car, rather than the amount of the debt, over the life of the plan. This is similar to redemption in a Chapter 7, but better because you don't have to pay the value of the car immediately in cash.

There are special limitations on your power to modify home mortgages, even in a Chapter 13, and these will be discussed in detail in Chapter 9, "Home Sweet Home." But you can still cure, or make up, any back payments over the life of the plan and start making regular payments again when you file.

Rent-to-Own Contracts

In the section on consensual liens in Chapter 6 we discussed purchase-money security interests, where you borrow money to buy a specific item and grant the seller or lender a security interest in that item. Rent-to-own contracts are similar, but they are really leases that have different legal consequences. With these contracts you lease a specific item, make "rent" payments, and end up owning it at the end of the contract. If a transaction is a "lease," the only way to keep the item is to make all the payments. You can't redeem the property in Chapter 7, and you can't just pay its value in Chapter 13 (although in a Chapter 13 you could make up back payments and make all future payments on time). Many lenders are wise to this and try to call transactions "leases" when they are really security interests. Most courts say that a transaction is not truly a lease unless you are allowed to cancel the deal at any time and return the merchandise without further obligation. Your lawyer should examine the fine print to see if a transaction is a true lease or a cleverly disguised security interest.

Truth-in-Lending Laws

So far, we've been discussing avoidance powers provided under the Bankruptcy Code. There's another federal law that gives you the power to cancel liens on your home. It's called the Truth in Lending Act (TILA).

If you borrow money against your home, the TILA gives you a three-day "cooling off" period to cancel the transaction, and the lender has to give you written notice that you have this right. TILA also requires that the lender give written disclosure of finance and other charges connected with your loan.

If a lender doesn't make the required disclosures in connection with a nonpurchase money loan, you can rescind the transaction at any time within the following three years, or when you sell your home, whichever comes first.

Outside of bankruptcy, a consumer who wants to cancel the lien against his or her home under TILA must give the money he or she received back to the lender. But when a consumer files bankruptcy, some courts have said that the lien can be canceled even though the loan is wiped out.

When Archie got a $22,000 home equity loan, he agreed to pay a $3,000 fee to the lender's agent for arranging the loan. The lender violated the TILA by not including this fee in the "finance charge" category on the disclosure statement. Two years later, when the lender called the loan, Archie's lawyer gave notice he was "rescinding" the loan and filed a Chapter 13 for Archie. The bankruptcy court canceled the mortgage and wiped out the debt.

Many states also have truth-in-lending laws that may be even more beneficial. Some give the debtor even more than three years to cancel. You should discuss with your lawyer any possible rescission rights under truth-in-lending laws. Although the lawyer may charge extra to look into the matter, it might be money well spent.

A creditor discovered Joan's little maneuver in public records and brought it to the court's attention. Joan had to transfer the home to the bankruptcy trustee, none of her debts were wiped out, and she barely missed going to jail.

8

· ·

CARS AND
HOUSEHOLD GOODS

Jake was kind of an eclectic, easygoing dude who didn't spend much time worrying about things like income taxes. He wasn't tempted by the usual trappings, like a home or a car, and surely wasn't the marrying kind. All he really cared about was his beloved Harley-Davidson motorcycle, but the IRS was about to seize his "hog" for nonpayment of income taxes. Good thing Jake knew his way to bankruptcy court.

What happens to your car and household goods when you file bankruptcy? As with everything else in bankruptcy law, and perhaps law in general, the answer is: it depends. Over the next few pages, we will address the variety of conditions and situations that govern your personal property.

This chapter includes:

- a recap of the legal principles that affect how your possessions are treated in bankruptcy
- some examples of how these principles apply to specific situations involving your car and your household belongings.

LEGAL PRINCIPLES AFFECTING YOUR POSSESSIONS

If you've read and remember the previous chapters, you might want to skip ahead to the sections on automobiles or household goods. Otherwise, take note of the following:

96

• There are three people who can have an interest in any of your assets: you (to the extent of any exemption), a secured creditor (to the extent of the secured debt), and the trustee (as to any remaining value in the asset).

• Your equity in an asset is determined by deducting the amount of any liens from its value.

• If an asset is subject to a security interest, but all of your equity is exempt, you can redeem it in a Chapter 7 by making a lump sum payment to the secured creditor equal to the value of the asset, continuing regular payments, or making payments under a reaffirmation agreement.

• In a Chapter 13 you can, in essence, "redeem" by paying the value of the property over the life of the plan. Or you can just continue to make the regular payments.

• In a Chapter 13 you can reinstate defaulted loans by making up missed payments over the life of the plan. In a Chapter 7 you have to make up back payments immediately after filing unless the creditor agrees otherwise.

• You can surrender the asset to the creditor and discharge the debt.

• The Bankruptcy Code gives you the power to avoid nonpurchase money security interests in household goods and tools of the trade.

• The automatic stay prevents secured creditors from repossessing your property, or selling it if it has already been repossessed.

• If you have nonexempt equity in an asset, a Chapter 7 trustee can sell the property, although he or she must pay you the amount of your exemption. In a Chapter 13, the trustee cannot sell the asset, but under the "best interests" test (see chapter 3, "Chapter 13 Defined") your plan payments will be higher because you have to pay creditors the value of any nonexempt property over the life of the plan.

AUTOMOBILES

Now, let's apply these principles to several specific examples involving automobiles and discuss your options. In all the following examples, the value of the car is $10,000, and the allowable exemption is $1,500.

Example 1: All the Equity Is Exempt,
and Loan Payments Are Current

Assume that you owe $9,000. Since you don't have any nonexempt equity, the trustee is not in the picture. You could surrender the car to the bank and wipe out the debt, or you could keep the car by just continuing to make the regular payments. But remember, in some states you must reaffirm even if payments are current.

In this example there is no advantage to a Chapter 13.

Example 2: All the Equity Is Exempt,
but You Are Behind in Payments

In this situation Chapter 13 offers the advantage of allowing you to make up the payments over the life of the Chapter 13 plan.

In a Chapter 7 the creditor might agree to allow you to make up back payments, but doesn't have to. It would be nice if you could discuss this matter with the creditor before you file bankruptcy, but watch out: if the creditor learns that you are about to file, it may try to snatch your car before you file your petition.

Another alternative would be to file a Chapter 7 and negotiate with the creditor after the automatic stay goes into effect. If the creditor refused to allow payments over time, you could convert from Chapter 7 to Chapter 13, and then you wouldn't need the creditor's consent.

Example 3: You Owe More Than the Car Is Worth

If you owed $11,000 on the car, the same rules would apply, except that in a Chapter 7 you could "redeem" by making a lump sum payment of $10,000. Obviously, that is not very realistic.

More realistically, you could pay $10,000 over the life of a Chapter 13 plan instead of paying the whole amount of the debt.

Example 4: You Have Nonexempt Equity in One Car

Assume that you owe only $6,000. You would then have nonexempt equity of $2,500 ($10,000 – $6,000 – $1,500).

In a Chapter 7 the trustee could sell the car, pay the creditor off, pay you $1,500 for your exemption, and distribute the rest to unsecured creditors.

In a Chapter 13 the trustee could not sell the car, but you would have to include the $2,500 nonexempt equity in your plan payments.

There is a third option, but it's tricky. Remember, some amount of prebankruptcy planning is allowed, but if you go too far your discharge might be denied. However, if you are willing to take the risk, you could: sell the car; buy another vehicle worth only $1,500; and take the balance of the proceeds ($2,500), which would otherwise be nonexempt, and make a couple of house payments (if your home equity is wholly exempt). Or you could pay some nondischargeable taxes, buy food or whatever before filing bankruptcy.

But don't try to sell the car to a friend for less than it's worth. That would be a fraudulent transfer, and it would definitely put your discharge at risk.

Example 5: You Have More Than One Car and Don't File Bankruptcy with Your Spouse

Your options are the same as above, except that you will have to choose which car to claim as exempt. Generally, states will allow you only one car exemption. Consequently, if you had $500 equity in one car and $700 in another car, you could lose one to a Chapter 7 trustee. In a Chapter 13, the value of one of the cars would increase your plan payments.

Other options include selling one car and spending the money, as discussed above, or selling both cars and using the proceeds to buy a single car, making sure that the value is within the amount of the exemption.

Example 6: You and Your Spouse File Jointly

The same rule applies if you and your spouse each own a car. If you have only one car, and it's jointly owned, some states allow you to combine your exemptions to protect equity up to $3,000.

HOUSEHOLD GOODS

For the most part, the rules pertaining to automobiles apply to your household goods, except that the Bankruptcy Code gives you the right to avoid nonpurchase money security interest in household goods.

There's also a practical difference when you are behind in payments on a purchase money security interest. With household goods, the secured creditor in a Chapter 7 will almost always allow you to make up back payments under a reaffirmation agreement. Unlike automobiles, there is little market for used household goods, so the creditor would much rather work with you to establish a repayment plan than seize the property and then have to deal with the problem of selling it.

Consider the following examples, which assume that the allowable exemption for household goods is $1,000.

Example 1: The Value of Your
Household Goods Is Less Than $1,000

There are no secured creditors to deal with, and the trustee has no interest in your household goods because their value is less than the exemption.

Example 2: A Creditor Holds a Purchase Money
Security Interest in Exempt Household Goods

Assume your household goods—worth only $1,000—include a refrigerator purchased from a department store. Odds are that the store has a purchase money security interest in the refrigerator, because of language contained in the charge account paperwork. (The trustee has no such interest in the goods because they are all exempt, but you will have to deal with the store.) Let's say you owe $800 on a refrigerator worth only $300.

You have three options, which, as a practical matter, can be accomplished in either a Chapter 7 or a Chapter 13:

- surrender the refrigerator and wipe out the debt
- pay the full amount of the debt under the terms of the original credit agreement
- redeem the refrigerator by paying $300.

Note that in a Chapter 7 you would have to make a lump sum payment soon after you file; in a Chapter 13 you could pay the $300 over the life of the plan.

Example 3: ABC Finance Company
Has a Nonpurchase Money Security Interest

Assume the same facts as in example 1(b), but add a $5,000 debt to ABC Finance Company, which has a security interest in all your household goods. The result is exactly the same as in example 1(b) because you could avoid the security interest of the finance company in either Chapter 7 or Chapter 13.

Example 4: You Have Nonexempt Assets
but No Security Interests

Let's say your household goods are worth $1,400 and you have a big-screen TV, owned free and clear, worth $800. Here, you would have to choose how you want to allocate your exemption or, as discussed above, sell some of the items and spend the money wisely before bankruptcy.

Example 5: You Have Household Goods
Exceeding the Exemption and Have Given ABC
Finance a Nonpurchase Money Security Interest in
Your Household Goods to Secure a Loan of $5,000

Your ability to avoid the security interest of the finance company is limited because the Bankruptcy Code allows avoidance only to the extent that the nonpurchase money security interest impairs your exemption. Since the value of your goods is more than the exemption, in either a Chapter 7 or a Chapter 13 you would have to choose which household goods you wanted to free from the lien. The finance company's security interest in the remaining property would also have to be dealt with.

If, for instance, you decided to avoid the security interest in all the goods except your $800 big-screen television, the TV would remain subject to the security interest and your options would be the same as in other cases of nonavoidable security interests:

- surrender the TV and wipe out the debt
- reaffirm the debt (which in this case would be crazy because you would be agreeing to pay $5,000 for an $800 television)
- pay the creditor the value of the TV—$800—in a lump sum (Chapter 7) or over time (Chapter 13).

Unlike the situation in example 4, you could not sell off some of the items before bankruptcy because they would be subject to the security interest.

> Chapter 13 was just the ticket for Jake. He got the IRS off his back, was allowed to pay his taxes—without interest or penalties—over three years. And most important, Jake and his Harley-Davidson are still together, til death do them part.

9

. . . .

HOME SWEET HOME

Like many couples, Dan and Jennifer lived from paycheck to paycheck. But when Dan fell off a ladder and broke his leg, he couldn't work for three months, and Jennifer's salary wasn't enough to put food on the table and pay the mortgage, so they slipped behind in the house payments. Later, when Dan got back on his feet, they dutifully resumed their payments, but the bank still tried to foreclose because of three missed payments.

Home ownership is such an integral part of the American Dream that lawmakers recognize the need to set up special rules to protect both lenders and borrowers. To encourage lending, Congress limits the ways in which mortgage debts can be altered through bankruptcy. To encourage and protect home ownership, special state and federal statutes allow debtors to shield their homestead from creditors.

Although many of the rules pertaining to cars and household goods also apply to your home, especially in bankruptcy cases filed under Chapter 7, home mortgages are afforded special treatment in Chapter 13. One of those advantages is the ability to make up missed payments under a palatable schedule without losing your home, and possibly reduce the amount of the loan.

In short, your homestead exemption protects all or a part of the value of your home in either Chapter 7 or Chapter 13. In addition, special provisions in Chapter 13 give you up to five years to make up back payments.

In this chapter, we:

- review some of the ground rules discussed in earlier chapters
- offer advice on making the difficult decision to keep or surrender your home
- tell you how to keep your home if that is your choice
- illustrate your options with a number of examples
- introduce you to the concept of *bifurcation*
- uncover a hidden serpent that may be lurking in the fine print of your mortgage.

REVIEW OF GROUND RULES PERTAINING TO HOMES

As we noted, Congress wants to encourage lenders to make home mortgages, so it tries to simultaneously limit the risk faced by banks and other lending institutions that make these sometimes hefty loans while still protecting the borrower.

It seeks to meet these twin objectives by: decreeing that folks who fall behind on home mortgages can avoid foreclosure by making up these payments gradually under a Chapter 13 plan; and establishing that home mortgages generally should not be otherwise modified in bankruptcy and that payments falling due after the petition must be made on time.

Let's take a look at the implications. First, there are three types of people who might have a financial interest in your home (keep in mind that equity is the difference between the value of the property and the amount of any liens that encumber it):

- you, to the extent of your homestead exemption
- secured creditors, including mortgage holders and other lien holders, such as judgment creditors
- the trustee, as to any remaining value in the residence.

A good starting point in determining value is the real property tax assessment. If your home was purchased recently, the price you paid for the home is also an indication of its value.

Be wary of estimates from real estate brokers; they may be inclined to overstate the value of your home in hopes of landing a job.

Some important observations:

• Liens that should be deducted from the value of the property to determine your equity include home mortgages, real estate taxes, federal tax liens, and judgment liens.

• Judgment liens can be avoided to the extent they impair your homestead exemption.

• Once you file bankruptcy, the automatic stay stops any further foreclosure proceedings until the creditor can get court permission to proceed.

• Even in Chapter 13, if you fail to keep up with postpetition payments on a residential mortgage, the court will grant the creditor permission to foreclose.

• If you have nonexempt equity in your home, a Chapter 7 trustee can sell the property if he or she pays you the amount of your homestead exemption.

• In a Chapter 13 the trustee cannot sell your home, but your plan payments will be higher because you have to pay creditors the value of the nonexempt equity over the life of the plan.

• *Real property* includes land and buildings.

• *Personal property* is everything that isn't real property. Some courts deem mobile homes real property and others consider them personal property.

• In a bankruptcy situation you always have the option of surrendering your home and discharging the debt.

• If you are behind in house payments on the petition date, you can make up the payments over the life of a Chapter 13 plan. However, in a Chapter 7 you would have to bring the payments current soon after the petition date, or the court would give the creditor permission to begin or continue foreclosure.

• If you have substantial equity in your home, you don't want a creditor to foreclose because foreclosure will usually destroy your homestead exemption. In most states homesteads are not protected against consensual liens.

• Foreclosure proceedings result in an auction of your home—and the price bid is rarely more than the amount necessary to pay off the mortgage. The buyer at such a sale acquires the property free of your homestead claim.

• State law determines whether your home qualifies as a homestead, and the rules vary.

• Again, mobile homes qualify as a homestead in some states but not in others. Also, there are special rules covering various circumstances, such as whether you must actually live on the property or what happens if you rent it out or have agreed to sell it.

The question of whether your property qualifies as a homestead depends on the status of the property on the petition date. But if you convert your case from Chapter 13 to Chapter 7, the status of the property is reexamined as of the date of the conversion. In other words, your property might have qualified as a homestead when your Chapter 13 was filed, but if you moved out of the property and then converted to Chapter 7, the property may no longer qualify as a homestead and the property would go to the trustee.

Finally, keep in mind that a well-publicized glitch in the Bankruptcy Code—one that wreaked havoc on condominium associations—has been eliminated by the 1994 amendments. Previously, people who owned a condominium or co-op could simply stop paying common charges (e.g., maintenance fees, utility charges, landscaping costs) and continue to live in the unit, or even rent it out, while bankruptcy proceedings were pending.

No more. As part of the 1994 reform package, Congress said that a debtor who doesn't surrender a condo or co-op after filing bankruptcy must pay all such charges that fall due after the petition date.

NO EQUITY?

If there is little or no equity in your home, the best choice might be to file under Chapter 7 and allow the mortgage holder to foreclose. Then there is no point in making further payments, provided that you have someplace to go and the funds to do so.

The creditor will, of course, foreclose, but so what? That usually takes three months—minimum—and often much longer. Meanwhile, you can continue living in the house, rent free.

Sometimes, the creditor will be willing to pay you something for a *deed in lieu of foreclosure* so that it can avoid the expense of foreclosure. In this situation you relinquish your interest in the property in exchange for a modest payment, perhaps $1,000, and also agree to move out within a specific time period. It's a tempting offer, but don't take it without first exploring the income tax consequences of such a "sale."

This is a time to bite the bullet and really be honest with yourself. If the mortgage payments are more than you can afford, they might drag you down again after your bankruptcy. If this is the case, let the house go. It may be painful at first, but you'll eventually be glad you did.

If you decide to surrender a condo or co-op, you can avoid nondischargeable postpetition assessments by surrendering the property as soon as possible after, or even before, filing bankruptcy.

Still, you might want to keep your home even though it isn't worth more than you owe against it right now if you think the value will appreciate, or if you are worried about finding a place to live after your bankruptcy.

KEEPING YOUR HOME IN CHAPTER 7

Chapter 7 is the best bet for keeping your home if *each* of the following requirements is met:

- mortgage payments are current
- the property qualifies as a homestead
- all your equity is exempt.

KEEPING YOUR HOME IN CHAPTER 13

Chapter 13 is the ticket if:

- you are behind in payments, or
- the property does not qualify as a homestead, or
- your equity in the property exceeds the amount covered by the allowable exemption.

Special Restrictions on Modifying Home Mortgages

If a creditor's only collateral is the mortgage on your principal residence, your power to modify the terms of the debt is limited to making up back payments under the plan and continuing to make all future regular monthly payments after the petition date.

Most important, if the special restrictions apply, bifurcation (splitting a claim into two distinct parts) is not an option. We'll discuss this powerful tool later in this chapter.

Back Payments. The Bankruptcy Code requires that back payments on residential mortgages be brought current within a "reasonable time" under the Chapter 13 plan. Some courts have said that back payments must be brought current in the early stages of the plan. Most, however, say they can be stretched over the full three to five years.

Previously, the special restrictions on modifying home mortgages required that you pay off the arrearage by the time the last regular mortgage payment was due. This created a problem for people whose mortgage had less than five years remaining. The 1994 amendments give folks in this predicament a break.

In other words, let's say you are $5,000 behind on a home mortgage with only two years remaining. Under the old law the balance would have to be paid off over the two years, not the three to five years of a bankruptcy plan. Now you can stretch the payments over the life of your Chapter 13 schedule.

Your Chapter 13 plan could:

- propose to suspend payments until you could sell the property to pay off the secured claim, or
- restructure the debt and reduce the interest rate, or
- reduce the balance of the loan through bifurcation (see discussion later in this chapter).

Home Mortgages Not Entitled to Special Protection

To avoid going overboard in protecting lenders, Congress imposed a number of conditions that must be satisfied to qualify a mortgage for special protection:

- the home must be the creditor's only security interest
- the loan must be secured by real property
- the real property must be the borrower's "principal" residence.

Hence the following mortgages would not be entitled to special protection:

Mortgages with Additional Collateral. Some lenders make a practice of requiring additional security interests in either your car or household goods when they make the loan. They think this gives them more leverage in forcing you to pay.

Not necessarily. If the lender got a security interest in your $100 junk car, in addition to the home mortgage, it lost the special protection for residential mortgages—a perfect example of the old adage: "Pigs get fat; hogs get slaughtered."

If a mortgage holder suspects that you are about to file bankruptcy, it may try to improve its position by giving up the additional collateral. This is one gift horse you should definitely look in the mouth. Check with your lawyer before accepting a release of collateral.

Mortgages on Mobile Homes Deemed Personal Property. If your state deems mobile homes personal property, as opposed to real property, loans secured by mobile homes are not entitled to residential mortgage protection.

Mortgages That Are Not on Principal Residences. A creditor with a lien on a vacation home or rental property would not be entitled to special treatment.

Sometimes the question arises as to when the "character" of the property is determined. For example, what if the property was rental property when you borrowed the money, but it was your principal residence when you filed bankruptcy?

The courts differ, but the most logical approach is to determine the nature of the property at the time when the loan was made. Then it wouldn't make any difference if you moved into or out of the property later.

Residences Used to Produce Income

Mortgages on income-producing property don't enjoy the special protection given to home mortgages. But what if you live there as well? A duplex would be a good example. Or what if you conduct business from your home? The courts disagree, but many say that the property is not "solely" a residence, so the special protections do not apply.

Second Mortgages

The above restrictions, if they are applicable, protect second mortgages the same as first mortgages, so your options are precisely the same. You must make, or cure, back payments over the life of the plan, and you must make all future monthly payments.

But a growing number of courts are saying that a second mortgage is not entitled to special protection if it is completely unsecured. For example, if your home is worth $50,000 and you owe $52,000 on a first mortgage, any second mortgage would, in effect, be unsecured. Under this scenario you could probably eliminate the second mortgage altogether in Chapter 13.

JOINTLY HELD PROPERTY

In the situation where spouses own property jointly, but only one person files bankruptcy, the courts disagree on how to figure the value of a one-half interest.

To illustrate the problem, assume your house is worth $90,000, mortgaged for $60,000, and that your state law allows a $20,000 homestead exemption. Some courts would value your one-half interest as follows:

• First, the mortgage is deducted from the value of the property: $90,000 – $60,000 = $30,000.
• This figure is then divided in half, so the value of your interest is $15,000.
• After deducting your exemption of $20,000, there is no value left for the estate.

If you and your spouse filed jointly, the estate *would* have an interest: $90,000 – $60,000 = $30,000, less the exemption of $20,000. That leaves a $10,000 value for the estate.

The court can authorize the trustee to sell the entire interest in the property and pay the nonfiling spouse the value of his or her interest, but judges are reluctant to wield that power. So in most cases when only one spouse files, the trustee is faced with the difficult task of selling the one-half interest. And even if he or she can find someone to buy a half interest, the nonfiling spouse has the right of first refusal.

The rules are different—and even more complicated—if you live in one of the nine community property states: Arizona, California, Idaho, Louisiana, Nevada, New Mexico, Texas, Washington, or Wisconsin. In these states even the nondebtor's interest in community property becomes property of the estate. If the community property is not fully covered by an exemption, it can be sold by the trustee (although only creditors with claims against both spouses would have a claim to the proceeds). Your home would be community property if it was obtained during the marriage, unless one spouse inherited the real estate.

To make matters even more complicated, some states recognize an ancient form of property ownership by a husband and wife called *tenancy by the entirety*. This means that creditors of only one spouse may not seize property owned by both spouses.

The effect of such a rule is that under some circumstances, jointly owned property might be fully exempt when only one spouse files bankruptcy in one of the following jurisdictions: Delaware, District of Columbia, Florida, Hawaii, Indiana, Maryland, Massachusetts, Michigan, Mississippi, Missouri, North Carolina, Ohio, Pennsylvania, Rhode Island, Vermont, Virginia, and Wyoming.

The main point to remember is that there may be real advantages in not filing a joint petition. Be sure to ask your lawyer to consider this possibility.

CAUTION! If you own property solely in your name, do not try to put it in the names of both you and your spouse without first talking to a bankruptcy lawyer. This could be considered a fraudulent transfer, creating serious consequences. (See the section on fraudulent transfers in chapter 7, "Games People Play," for a more detailed discussion.)

JUDGMENT LIENS

Judgments entered against you in many courts result in a lien against all your real property. Judgment liens are a hassle because, even if avoided as impairing your homestead, they continue to haunt your effort to build up equity in the property, and they also reattach or recur. Congress made an attempt to fix that glitch with the 1994 amendments, but it remains to be seen whether that effort will succeed. (If you are facing a judgment, you might want to refer back to chapter 7, particularly the section on judgment liens.)

In any case where you intend to keep your home, your bankruptcy petition should be filed before any judgments are entered against you.

Also, remember that under the 1994 amendments child support and alimony judgments entered by divorce courts before bankruptcy cannot be avoided. But it's not clear if judgments securing property divisions are protected.

CURE: MAKING BACK PAYMENTS

Cure refers to the process of making up back mortgage payments during the course of a Chapter 13 case. Courts disagree on when it is too late to cure.

What is clear, however, is that you can't cure if the foreclosure has been completed, the property has been sold, and any redemption rights have been extinguished. Equally clear is that you can cure if foreclosure proceedings have just been started. But there are myriad points in between where the courts differ.

The 1994 amendments clear up some of the confusion, for people who file on or after October 22, 1994, by saying that they can cure until the property is actually sold at a foreclosure sale.

But even if you don't file bankruptcy before the foreclosure sale, you still may have redemption rights under state law. (Don't confuse these with the right to redeem personal property under the Bankruptcy Code. This kind of redemption is discussed in chapters 7 and 8.)

Most states allow a period of time, usually six months to a year, to redeem real property, even after it is sold at foreclosure. But note the difference between redemption and cure. When you cure, you just have to make up the missed payments; you don't have to pay the whole loan. And you can take up to five years to make up the back payments.

Redemption, on the other hand, requires that you pay the whole loan, and you can't stretch payments over the life of the plan. The whole thing has to be paid before the redemption period expires.

This is pretty complicated stuff, but the important thing to remember is to contact a bankruptcy lawyer as soon as possible after foreclosure proceedings are started. Then you can learn the deadlines and plan accordingly.

BIFURCATION

Bifurcation, meaning "division into two parts," comes into play in bankruptcy only in Chapter 13 cases. It allows a secured claim to be split—a tremendous benefit in bankruptcy and a wonderful legal asset if you know how to take advantage of it.

To backtrack a bit, remember that a loan can be both secured and unsecured at the same time. The bifurcation issue arrises because a debt is secured only to the value of the collateral. The general rule in Chapter 13 is that secured claims must be paid at least the value of the security (if you want to keep the collateral), but unsecured claims can be paid little or nothing.

Let's consider a practical application of that rather arcane principle. Assume your property is worth $75,000, but a creditor has a mortgage for $100,000. The creditor has two claims: a secured claim equal to the value of the collateral, or $75,000; and an unsecured claim for the balance, which is $25,000. The claim can be bifurcated by dividing the $100,000 claim into a secured claim of $75,000 and an unsecured claim of $25,000. If your plan, like many, proposes only nominal payments to unsecured creditors, bifurcation enables you to reduce the principal amount due on your mortgage from $100,000 to $75,000.

Not bad!

As usual, however, it's not always quite that easy. If the claim is entitled to the special protection for residential mortgages, bifurcation is not allowed. So, without the benefit of bifurcation, the whole $100,000 would have to be treated as a secured claim and paid in accordance with the loan documents—rather than just the $75,000.

But let's say that when the bank made the loan for your mortgage, it also took a security interest in your $100 junk car. That decision— and it's not all that unusual—would cause the bank to lose the special protection for residential mortgages. It would also cost the lending institution $25,000 if the borrower filed Chapter 13.

Usually, lenders of first mortgages won't lend more than the property is worth. But lenders of second mortgages are more inclined to take the plunge (although typically for smaller amounts).

As indicated earlier, if your home is not worth more than the first mortgage, the second mortgage is not protected and may be eliminated. But if your property is worth as little as one dollar more than the amount due on the first mortgage, the entire second mortgage is protected and must be paid if you want to keep your home.

DUE-ON-SALE CLAUSES: A SLEEPING GIANT

You may have a monster lurking in the fine print of your mortgage, and it may cause you to lose your home if:

- you assumed an existing loan when you bought your house, rather than obtaining your own financing, or
- there is a lien—such as a second mortgage, judgment, or tax lien—that attached to your home since the mortgage was signed.

If neither of those conditions apply to you, you're out of the woods. However, if either does apply, you may have a problem.

A *due-on-sale clause* is a provision buried in the fine print of many mortgages. It says that if the property is sold or liens attach to it, the entire loan becomes due immediately. Generally, nobody pays any attention to these clauses—not even the lender—and they are routinely violated. The lender usually ignores them so long as somebody is making the payments, even if that person is not the original borrower.

Recently, however, a few mortgage creditors have been scouring loan documents searching for due-on-sales problems. If the creditor learns that you've allowed a lien to attach to the property, it might try to claim that the loan is in default in a way that Chapter 13 has no mechanism to cure. So far, the courts are siding with the creditors on this one.

Until and unless the courts or Congress put this monster to rest, it is essential that a lawyer carefully examine your mortgage documents for any possible violation of a due-on-sale clause. If there is a violation, you have to seriously consider whether it's wise to alert the lender.

EXAMPLES

Bankruptcy statutes on homes and home ownership are among the most complicated in the law and among the most difficult for lawyers and nonlawyers to follow. Here are some examples that, we hope, will make them a little easier to understand.

For these examples, assume that your residence is worth $100,000, and your state allows $20,000 as a homestead exemption. Unless otherwise stated, also assume that the mortgage qualifies for the special Chapter 13 protection that we discussed earlier and that bifurcation is not an option.

Example 1: No Equity/Payments Current

You owe $120,000 on your mortgage but are current on all payments. The mortgage payments didn't push you to bankruptcy; $50,000 in medical and credit card bills did the trick.

In either a Chapter 7 or a Chapter 13, you could continue to make payments and keep your house. Since the house is worth less than you owe, consider surrendering it. Ask yourself whether the payments are realistic or a burdensome albatross that will drag you down again after bankruptcy. Remember, if you choose to give up the house, you can live there rent free at least three months while a foreclosure proceeds.

In this scenario there is no advantage to a Chapter 13, only disadvantages. There is the obvious burden of committing to a long-term payment plan, plus the added cost of a Chapter 13. Attorney fees will be higher, but the bigger concern might be the trustee's commissions.

A trustee charges a commission of up to 10 percent annually on payments made through the plan. In this example, if regular payments are made through the plan, the trustee's commissions can run as high as $1,000 for every year of the plan. That's a pretty steep price.

Fortunately, many courts will allow you to make regular mortgage payments outside the plan, as long as payments are current on the petition date. Whenever possible, your plan should propose that payments be made directly to the mortgage holder, rather than through the trustee. Discuss this option with your lawyer. For obvious reasons, the trustee might not mention it.

Example 2: Special Restrictions
on Bifurcation Not Applicable

Assume the same facts as in example 1, plus the fact that the bank also took a security interest in your $200 car. This example illustrates the importance of determining whether the Chapter 13 restrictions on modifying residential mortgages apply to your loan.

Since the bank has a security interest in the clunker car, the loan is not secured "solely"—as required—by your principal residence. So the restrictions don't apply. Consequently, you could reduce the principal balance on the loan from $120,000 to $100,200 (value of car plus value of home). Although that wouldn't reduce the payments, it would shorten the term for the simple reason that the amount due has been reduced by $19,800.

Example 3: No Equity/Payments Behind

Assume the same facts as in example 1, but instead of being current in payments, you fell $5,000 behind trying to keep up with the medical and credit card bills.

If you want to keep your house, contact the bank and ask if it would voluntarily agree to allow you to make up the payments over time. If so, Chapter 7 would be your best bet. With a Chapter 7, you could discharge the medical and credit card bills and, with the bank's consent, make up the back payments over time.

Unfortunately, most lenders won't agree to this, so you have to force it on them—by filing a Chapter 13. (Like example 1, this example assumes the bank loan qualifies for the special protection given to residential mortgages in Chapter 13. If these restrictions did not apply, you could reduce the balance of your mortgage as discussed above.)

In some jurisdictions the Chapter 13 trustee pays arrearages in the beginning of the plan and unsecured claims after the arrearages are paid in full. So if, in this example, the only reason for filing a Chapter 13, rather than a Chapter 7, was that the bank wouldn't give you time to make up the back payments of $5,000, you might be able to wait until the arrearages are paid by the trustee and then convert your case to Chapter 7. If your Chapter 13 was filed on or after October 22, 1994—so that the 1994 amendments apply—this would appear to be a sound strategy, but be sure to discuss it thoroughly with your lawyer.

Example 4: Equity Within Exemption/Payments Current

You owe $85,000 on your mortgage, and payments are current. Since your equity of $15,000 ($100,000 − $85,000) is less than your homestead exemption, the trustee has no interest in your home. Just the same, you have substantial equity that you would probably lose if the bank foreclosed.

If you want to keep the house, just continue to make your regular mortgage payments. There is no advantage here to a Chapter 13, at least as far as your house is concerned. Bifurcation, even if available, would not help you in this instance because the house is worth more than the mortgage.

If you don't want to keep the house, but do want to preserve your equity, you should continue to make the regular payments and try to sell it. In a typical Chapter 7, the automatic stay lasts for about four months. After this, you could sell the house, and, if you were behind in payments, the bank could start foreclosure proceedings, which usually take a good three months.

Example 5: Equity Within Exemption/Payments Behind

Assume the same facts as in example 4, except that instead of being current on your mortgage, you are $5,000 behind in payments.

In this situation the ramifications are similar to those in example 3, but you'll probably lose the $15,000 equity you've built up if the property is foreclosed.

Example 6: Foreclosure Proceedings Started

Assume the same facts as in example 5, plus the fact that the bank has already begun a mortgage foreclosure lawsuit against you.

If you want to save your home, you have only one option: file a Chapter 13 immediately. Call a lawyer and make sure that she or he knows that foreclosure proceedings have already been initiated.

Under the 1994 amendments you have at least until the foreclosure sale. But the sooner you file bankruptcy and stop the foreclosure, the less you'll have to pay to cure. This is because foreclosure costs, including the creditor's attorney fees, are usually added to the amount needed to cure.

Example 7: Effect of Judgment

You owe $85,000 on your mortgage, plus a creditor has sued you and obtained a judgment lien. In this example it doesn't make any difference whether you are current on your mortgage payments.

If it weren't for the judgment, you would have $15,000 equity in your home. Under either Chapter 7 or Chapter 13, you can "avoid" this judgment because it impairs your exemption. However, many courts have ruled that avoided judgment liens can linger while you build up nonexempt equity in the property.

So let's say five years down the road you've reduced the mortgage to $80,000 and its value has risen to $120,000. Your equity is now $40,000. Case law says that the judgment lien reattaches to your house.

In the 1994 amendments Congress tried to prevent judgment liens from reattaching in this situation, but it remains to be seen whether this goal was really achieved. Thus, it's better to file bankruptcy before a judgment is entered against you. If that's not possible, plan on replacing your current house as soon as your bankruptcy is over. That way the judgment lien will not attach to equity you build up in your new house.

Example 8: Equity Exceeds Exemption

The balance on your mortgage is $70,000, so your equity is $30,000. Since your homestead exemption is only $20,000, you have $10,000 of nonexempt equity.

In a Chapter 7 the trustee could sell your home, give you $20,000, pay off the mortgage, and hand over the balance to your unsecured creditors.

In a Chapter 13 you would have to pay back the $10,000 over the life of the plan. In theory, unsecured creditors are supposed to get the benefit of the $10,000 that they would have received in a Chapter 7.

Bearing in mind the risks, and after talking to your lawyer, you might be able to avoid losing the $10,000 in a Chapter 7 or having to repay it in a Chapter 13. For instance, you might want to replace the home with one where all the equity would be within the exemption. Then any surplus from the sale proceeds could be used to purchase other exemptions and for living expenses.

Another possibility, which would be allowed by some courts but disallowed by others, would be to take out a second mortgage for $10,000, thus eliminating the nonexempt equity, and using the money to buy other exempt assets. Of course, you will have to repay the second mortgage. This is an extremely aggressive strategy and should not be considered without thoroughly discussing it with an experienced bankruptcy attorney.

> Like a growing number of people, Dan and Jennifer were virtually pushed into bankruptcy by the foolish policy of their mortgage holder. As would be expected, they filed Chapter 13, the court protected their home and allowed them to make up the missed mortgage payments over three years. The lender got its money; Dan and Jennifer kept their house. And, thanks to sensible bankruptcy statutes, everybody's happy.

10

· ·

LIFE AFTER BANKRUPTCY

Leo thinks debtors are trashy deadbeats, so when Sue, his book-
keeper, had to seek financial relief in court, he schemed to get rid
of her. Leo knew he couldn't just fire Sue for filing bankruptcy, so
he started accumulating "other" reasons to give her the pink slip.

Congress wants you to get back on your feet and has enacted laws
to prevent creditors and others from stepping on your fingers as you
climb up the ladder of financial security.
This chapter addresses:

- laws protecting you from discrimination
- steps you can take to repair your credit
- special problems encountered in Chapter 13.

NONDISCRIMINATION LAWS

With passage of the 1994 amendments, the Bankruptcy Code
now contains three key antidiscrimination provisions. One of these
provisions says that your employer may not fire or discriminate
against you "solely" because you filed bankruptcy or failed to pay a
dischargeable debt. Another applies to governmental units. The third
provision forbids discrimination in making student loans. These provisions give you a substantial shield.

Employment Discrimination

Your employer cannot fire or discriminate against you in any way "solely" because you filed bankruptcy. But your employer may attempt to devise a trumped-up case against you to skirt the law. If you think that's happening, see a lawyer pronto—before your employer has a chance to document that you use the office copying machine for personal business or spend too much time at the water cooler.

Governmental Discrimination

In addition to keeping employers in check, the antidiscrimination provisions also apply to governmental units, forbidding bureaucrats from yanking privileges because you filed bankruptcy. In other words, the state can't take away your cosmetology or architectural license because you are seeking financial relief under the U.S. Bankruptcy Code.

Most states have laws suspending the driver's license of someone who fails to pay for damages caused with a motor vehicle. But the Bankruptcy Code overrules inconsistent state laws and requires the state to restore your driver's license when you show that liability for these damages was discharged in bankruptcy.

When Fred filed bankruptcy, his credit union at work wanted to suspend his privileges. No way, the court said. That's employment discrimination. The court ordered the credit union to restore Fred's rights.

Similarly, in many states your driver's license can be suspended for unpaid fines. If you discharge a fine in bankruptcy, the state should be required to restore your license, but local courts frequently try to figure out ways to get around this.

Student Loan Discrimination

Finally, as a result of the 1994 amendments, lenders who participate in government loan programs can no longer discriminate against applicants on the basis of a prior bankruptcy.

CREDIT REPAIR

$\mathcal{S}$ ince credit repair involves qualifying for and using new credit, the following discussion is applicable only if you file a Chapter 7 or if your Chapter 13 plan is completed. During a Chapter 13 case you are not allowed to incur any consumer credit without the trustee's consent. But once your Chapter 13 is complete, you can still use the fact that you faithfully adhered to the plan to show that you've learned to control your finances.

A study by the Credit Research Center at Purdue University shows that roughly one-third of the people who file for consumer bankruptcy obtain new lines of credit within three years. Fully half had credit restored within five years. Although bankruptcy remains on credit reports for ten years, there are some things you can do right away, especially in a Chapter 7, to start rebuilding. And as the Purdue University research shows, you can quickly reestablish your credit.

Credit repair requires that you create confidence in potential lenders of your ability and willingness to pay any new loan. You have to show that your bankruptcy wiped the slate clean, and that you've used postbankruptcy credit well. If you work at it, you can be well on the road to establishing good credit within a year after filing Chapter 7.

So there are two parts of the process: cleaning up your credit reports, and getting initial credit so you can establish a good postbankruptcy payment record.

Credit Reports

Like it or not, your ability to get credit is determined largely by credit reports issued by three huge, faceless corporations: CBI/Equifax, Trans Union, and TRW. These reports show who has extended credit to you, the amount, your payment record, and information from public records.

Where do the three corporations get this information? From either creditors or public records. Most major lenders and many small local ones "subscribe" to one or more of these credit bureaus. In return for receiving credit reports, these "subscribers" agree to furnish current information about your account.

Recent studies show that much of the information is flat-out wrong. About half of all credit reports contain errors—such as adverse information about someone with a similar name, duplicate accounts, and obsolete data. Unfortunately, it can be difficult to set things straight: subscribing creditors are the backbone of a credit bureau's business, so any time it comes down to your word versus the creditor's, you can guess which party the bureau is going to believe.

Unless a disputed item is a matter of public record, the credit bureau does not undertake any independent investigation; it merely asks the creditor to verify the information and takes that verification at face value. So if the creditor claims that the information is correct, it remains on your credit report.

The Fair Credit Reporting Act. Still, you do get some relief from the federal Fair Credit Reporting Act, which protects your right to:

- know what is in your credit file
- be informed of the name and address of any credit bureau issuing a credit report that caused you to be denied credit—and a free copy of that report
- learn who has received a copy of your credit report within the past six months
- force the credit bureau to verify any information that you claim is wrong, and to delete it if it cannot be verified within thirty days
- insist that corrected reports be sent to anyone who received an incorrect version within the past six months (within two years if the incorrect report was ordered for employment-related reasons)
- expunge adverse information after seven years (ten years for a bankruptcy)
- include a written statement in your credit file explaining any item that you dispute, but that the creditor insists is correct.

The FCRA gives consumers the right to sue in court or complain to the Federal Trade Commission, but, as a practical matter, your best tactic is probably polite persistence. While the credit bureaus have a natural bias in favor of subscribing creditors, company policy is always to comply with the law.

The first step in challenging an item is to complete the dispute form sent to you with your credit report. If the disputed item is not removed, you can at least prepare a written statement up to one hundred words explaining your side of the dispute. To be honest, this statement probably won't do any immediate good—most creditors are linked to credit bureaus by computer, and your statement is not transmitted with the credit report—but it does establish a record.

When you dispute an item that is not a matter of public record, it's best to also write to the creditor asking that it contact the credit bureau and correct the mistake.

All contact with a credit bureau or a creditor concerning a disputed item should be by certified letter, return receipt requested. This will more likely get their attention and will also build a good record. It will be much easier to get a lawyer to help you if there is a paper trail of your efforts requesting that the credit bureau comply with its obligations under the law.

Credit Reports After Bankruptcy. About six months after your discharge, you should order credit reports from each of the "big three." For instructions on ordering the reports, call the following numbers:

- Trans Union (800) 851-2674
- TRW (800) 392-1122
- CBI/Equifax (800) 685-1111.

Trans Union and CBI/Equifax charge $8 for each report, whereas TRW offers one free credit report per year.

The credit reports should show that you filed bankruptcy and received your discharge. All your prepetition accounts should show zero balances. If they don't, or if there are other mistakes, follow the instructions that come with your credit report for disputing items. Send in the dispute form (always through certified mail, return receipt requested), copies of your bankruptcy petition (schedules D, E, and F) showing all the debts you listed, and the court's Order of Discharge.

Be sure to specifically request a copy of the corrected report and insist that the same be distributed to all potential creditors who received the inaccurate version within the past six months (or within the past two years for a report requested for employment-related purposes).

New Credit

Once your postbankruptcy credit reports show a clean slate, you are halfway home—but only halfway. Now you have to establish a good payment record and have your good work reflected on the credit reports.

If you are continuing to make payments on a prepetition debt—such as a house or car—you are off to a good start.

The next step is to call Bankcard Holders of America at (703) 389-5445, which for a small fee will send you a list of banks offering "secured" credit cards. These banks will guarantee you a credit card so long as you keep enough money on deposit to pay the account. (In other words, if you have a $300 line of credit, you will need to keep $300 on deposit.) When signing up for one or more of these cards, however, confirm that the issuing bank will report your good payment history to the credit bureaus. Otherwise, you won't be accomplishing your aim of reestablishing credit worthiness.

You also might be able to find a bank or credit union that will give you a small loan if you maintain a certain balance in an account there, but before you actually apply, ask if the institution will report a good payment history to the credit bureaus.

Some people actually receive credit card solicitations immediately after bankruptcy from creditors who know that debtors have no other bills and cannot file bankruptcy again for six years. If you receive one of these solicitations, apply for the credit card but answer all the questions on the application truthfully. Also, used-car dealers will frequently offer credit immediately after bankruptcy.

Even if you are making payments to a creditor who doesn't report to the credit bureaus, you can still write the agencies yourself to ask that this information be included. The credit bureaus are not required to do this—and may turn you down—but it doesn't hurt to ask. Be sure to include the creditor's phone number and any account number so that the credit bureaus can verify the information. You also have the option, once you've established a good payment history, of asking the creditor to be a credit reference for you.

While it's important to start building a credit history, you should begin slowly. If you go wild and apply for credit all over the place, your report will probably show that you tried—and failed—to get credit. That makes lenders nervous, and they begin to think you are getting in trouble again or that there is some egregious problem that they are missing. In any case, they will be looking for an excuse to turn you down. Don't give them that excuse.

If You're Married . . .

A married person should try to establish credit in his or her own name and avoid joint accounts. That way, each person is responsible for building his or her own credit history.

The federal Equal Credit Opportunity Act (ECOA) and laws in many states say that a creditor cannot refuse to extend credit because of gender, marital status, race, religion, or age.

If you and your spouse already have a joint account and are building a good payment record, make sure that each person's credit reports reflect this good record. If not, write a letter to the creditor requesting that it report this favorable information to the credit bureaus—under both your name and the name of your spouse.

> Although Sue was a good employee—loyal, dependable, hardworking—and her financial troubles had nothing to do with her job, Leo fired her, ostensibly for incompetence, when he found out she had filed for bankruptcy protection. The court didn't believe his story for a second. Sue's boss learned the hard way that the laws of the United States won't tolerate that kind of discrimination. Leo had to give Sue back her job and pay her for the whole year she was out of work.

11

. . . .

YOU BLEW IT AGAIN?

The Chapter 13 repayment plan was working great for Phyllis and Tom. They were diligently making up the missed mortgage payments and, finally, could see some light at the end of the tunnel. Then their teenage son fractured his skull in a car crash, and Phyllis and Tom had to use the mortgage money for doctor bills. The bank wanted to foreclose on their house.

Okay, things got out of hand and you missed some Chapter 13 payments. What now?

Sometimes, even the best Chapter 13 plan falls through because the debtor gets fired or laid off, suffers illness, or is unable to make payments as a result of other unforeseen events. If this happens, all is not necessarily lost, but you should contact your lawyer immediately.

Depending on the type of payments involved, the options include:

- suspension of payments
- plan modification
- hardship discharge
- conversion to Chapter 7
- dismissal
- dismissal followed by a Chapter 7
- dismissal followed by a second Chapter 13.

Most Chapter 13 plans require a regular payment to the trustee, who applies it to any mortgage arrearages, taxes, car payments, and unsecured claims owed under the plan. Call these *trustee pay-ments.*

Some Chapter 13 plans also provide for additional payments to se-cured creditors *outside the plan.* Usually, these are mortgage and car payments coming due after the petition date.

TRUSTEE PAYMENTS

If you miss payments to the trustee, the court will dismiss your Chapter 13 and creditors will be free to resume collection efforts against you and your property. Additionally, you may be ineligible for either Chapter 13 or Chapter 7 relief for 180 days (see discussion of the 180-day rule later in this chapter).

Suspend Payments

If you miss payments because of a temporary crisis, the wise thing to do is to ask the court to allow you to suspend payments until the cri-sis is over. In that situation, the suspended payments are not for-given; they are just paid later, and the plan is extended for a longer period of time. Courts generally approve of this buffer, so long as you have a good reason and the judge is convinced the problem is truly temporary.

But there's a hitch. Remember that a Chapter 13 can run no longer than sixty months. If your plan is already at sixty months, you can't just suspend payments; the plan must be modified.

Plan Modification

If suspension of payments won't work—either because your change in circumstances is not temporary or because your plan is already sixty months long—it may be possible to modify the Chapter 13 plan. Usually, this will result in lower payments now and higher ones in the future. Of course, any proposed modification must be feasible, so the court will examine your situation to see if it's likely that you will be able to make higher payments at a later date.

If you can't suspend payments or afford higher future payments under a modified plan, consider asking the court for a hardship dis-charge.

Hardship Discharge

A hardship discharge stops the Chapter 13 plan in its tracks and excuses all remaining payments. To qualify for such a discharge, you must:

- convince the court that your inability to make payments is for reasons beyond your control
- show that modification of the plan is not feasible
- have made payments equal to the value of any nonexempt property you had on the petition date.

The major disadvantage of a hardship discharge is that you don't get the usual "super discharge" given in Chapter 13 cases. That means if a debt would not have been discharged in a Chapter 7, it will not be eliminated because of hardship.

> Abe filed Chapter 7 two years ago and, lo and behold, is in trouble again, with $10,000 in new credit card bills. Chapter 7 wasn't available, so he tried to make payments under Chapter 13. No dice. He just couldn't keep up. Abe's attorney convinced the court to award a hardship discharge. Once again, Abe's slate is clean.

Still, a hardship discharge has the following advantages over converting the case to Chapter 7:

- You are eligible for a hardship discharge even if you received a discharge in a bankruptcy case filed within six years of the petition date of your present Chapter 13. You would not be eligible for a Chapter 7 discharge.
- The property you owned when your Chapter 13 was filed will not be reexamined, as it would if you converted the case to Chapter 7. This can be an especially important issue if, for example, you moved out of your home (which had qualified for a homestead exemption) or the law governing exemptions was altered. If you converted to Chapter 7, the court could apply the new rules and your property might no longer be exempt. Not so with a hardship discharge.

Conversion to Chapter 7

In most cases a debtor has an absolute right either to convert a Chapter 13 to a Chapter 7, or to dismiss a Chapter 13 and file a brand-new Chapter 7.

An advantage of conversion over a hardship discharge is that debts arising after your Chapter 13 petition was filed can be included in the converted Chapter 7 case but would not be included in a hardship discharge.

The advantages of converting to Chapter 7 rather than dismissing a Chapter 13 and filing a new Chapter 7 are as follows:

• If you convert to Chapter 7, you retain the benefit of cramdown (where you pay the value of the collateral over time). If a Chapter 13 is dismissed, you will probably lose this benefit. For example, a plan may provide that the value of a car, say $5,000, is to be paid over the life of the plan. If you paid $3,000 toward the car in Chapter 13 and then converted to Chapter 7, all you would need to do to keep the vehicle is come up with the outstanding balance—$2,000. But if you dismissed the Chapter 13 and filed a new Chapter 7, the car would be appraised anew, and the redemption price could reflect the value on the date of the Chapter 7 filing, regardless of how much was paid in the earlier Chapter 13.

• Payments that the Chapter 13 trustee made to creditors cannot be set aside as preferences (see "Preferential Transfers" in chapter 7, "Games People Play") if the case is converted.

• Attorney fees and costs are usually a little less with a conversion than with a dismissal and refiling.

• The law may have changed after you filed your Chapter 13. If the change is not beneficial to you, a conversion would be better than filing a new case where the new law would be applied. For example, five-year-old student loans used to be dischargeable in a Chapter 7. Now they must be seven years old.

• If your Chapter 13 is governed by the 1994 amendments (filed on or after October 22, 1994), any assets you acquire and any increases in the value of your property that occur during the Chapter 13 remain yours and don't become part of the Chapter 7 estate if you convert; they would, however, become part of the estate in a new Chapter 7. If your Chapter 13 was filed before this date, these assets become property of the estate whether you convert or file a new case.

The disadvantages of converting over dismissing and refiling a Chapter 7 are as follows:

• Any funds held by the Chapter 13 trustee—money that was not paid out before your conversion to Chapter 7—will go to the Chapter 7 trustee when the case is converted. By contrast, if the case is dismissed, you get the money back. This is more significant than is readily apparent because most trustees disburse on a quarterly basis. But the 1994 amendments at least suggest that this money should be returned to you even if the case is converted to Chapter 7.

• If you convert to Chapter 7, you can't dismiss or reconvert to a Chapter 13. If you dismissed your Chapter 13 and then filed a new Chapter 7, you would have the option of converting it to a Chapter 13.

• You could not take advantage of favorable changes in the law, enacted after your Chapter 13 was initially filed.

Dismissal Followed by a New Chapter 13

Sometimes it's better to dismiss your Chapter 13 and start all over again, rather than modify your existing Chapter 13 plan.

The advantages:

• You get a brand-new sixty-month period to repay your debts. For example, if you were in the fourth year of a five-year plan when problems developed, you would only have the remaining one year to cure the problems. In a new Chapter 13, you would have a full sixty months.

• Debts incurred since filing of the original Chapter 13 could be included.

The disadvantages:

• If a Chapter 13 is dismissed, the benefit of cramdown will probably be lost. Example: A plan may provide that the value of a car, say $5,000, is to be paid over the life of the plan. If the Chapter 13 case is dismissed after you paid $3,000, you have to start all over again and pay the full value of the car over the life of the new Chapter 13.

• More restrictive laws enacted since your original Chapter 13 would apply in a new case.

• Whenever a debtor files more than one Chapter 13, the court looks very carefully at all the circumstances to determine whether the second case is filed in "bad faith."

• A Chapter 13 filed on or after October 22, 1994, is subject to new rules on payment of accrued alimony or child support. The new rules require that these obligations be paid in full over the life of the plan. If the back alimony or support is more than you could pay over five years, you may not be eligible for Chapter 13 under the new rules.

The 180-Day Rule

This rule forbids a second bankruptcy within 180 days of dismissal of an earlier case if dismissal:

• was requested by a debtor after a creditor asked the court for permission to foreclose (a motion for *relief from stay*), or
• was because a debtor intentionally failed to comply with a court order.

When a previous Chapter 13 case was dismissed because a debtor couldn't make plan payments, some courts ruled that the "180 days" doesn't apply, saying that the inability to make payments is not an intentional disregard of a court order. On the other hand, some courts forbid a refiling, and 180 days is enough time for an aggressive mortgage holder to foreclose on your house.

There is some inconsistency in how the courts apply this rule, but many won't use it when the dismissal is at the request of the trustee because of your inability to make plan payments.

PAYMENTS OUTSIDE THE PLAN

Many Chapter 13 plans provide that certain payments are made directly to secured creditors. The main reason for making these payments outside the plan is to avoid the trustee's commission.

Such payments are most frequently made on home mortgages and car loans.

Mortgage Payments

Many Chapter 13 plans provide that back mortgage payments owed on the petition date will be included in the payment to the trustee, and that all payments coming due after the petition date will be paid directly to the creditor outside the plan.

The trustee is primarily concerned with the payments that are supposed to come to him or her, so if those payments are current he or she usually will not take any action if you default in payments outside the plan. But under these circumstances the creditor will usually ask the court for relief from stay, permitting it to foreclose.

Basically, there are three options:

• You could choose to do nothing, in which case the court will probably grant the request and allow foreclosure proceedings to begin. (Obviously, you should choose this option only if you are prepared to let the property go. Still, the Chapter 13 plan should be modified to deal with any deficiency.)

• You could modify the plan to add the missed postpetition payments to the payments being made to the trustee, essentially treating them the same as missed prepetition payments. The major limitation is that there must be enough time left in the plan to cover the increased amount, or you must show that your income will increase enough so you can make higher payments in the future.

• Finally, if you have substantial equity in the property, the court may allow you a short time to sell the property and pay off the creditor. Although you don't get to keep the property, at least you will not lose your homestead exemption.

Remember that once the creditor asks the court for relief from the automatic stay, you run up against the 180-day rule. If you voluntarily dismiss your case after a motion for relief from the stay is filed, you can't refile for 180 days.

Drop-Dead Agreements. Sometimes, a mortgage lender will agree to withdraw its opposition to the automatic stay, provided you agree that any further missed payments will result in virtually automatic foreclosure. This Damocles sword, known as the *drop-dead agreement*—because if you blow it again, you're "dead"—is dangerous. But it may be your only option.

Ordinarily, your lawyer would negotiate the terms of such an agreement. But you should watch to make sure that everybody agrees on the date that payments must be made, the amount of the payments, and whether the payments are to be made directly to the creditor or to the trustee. Also, try to get the creditor to agree to give you notice and a short time—ten days is reasonable—to make up any payment you accidentally miss.

POSTPETITION DEBTS

If your budget was realistic, and there are no unforeseen catastrophes after confirmation of your Chapter 13 plan, you shouldn't need postpetition credit. In fact, as we said in the credit repair section of chapter 10, "Life After Bankruptcy," you are not supposed to incur any postpetition debts without the trustee's permission. But as a practical matter, it is occasionally necessary or wise to incur a new debt. However, doing so is potentially perilous and should be done only in consultation with your attorney and the trustee.

The implications of postpetition credit vary, depending on the type involved.

Nonemergency Postpetition Credit

The need for postpetition credit is a warning signal. Figure out what's going wrong before racking up new debts. If your budget was unrealistic, admit it and call your lawyer about modifying your plan. Otherwise, things are just going to get worse.

As we've said, postpetition debts may be dischargeable if you convert to Chapter 7 or dismiss your Chapter 13 and file a new case. But if you incurred debts during a Chapter 13—and didn't tell the creditor that you were in bankruptcy—that creditor has a pretty good argument that this debt should be excepted from discharge because of fraud.

But before concluding that you can't live within your budget, sit down and have a serious talk with yourself. Do you really need the credit to survive, or do you just need to exercise some spending discipline? Each time you say no to temptation, you take another step toward controlling your life and avoiding the old spending habits that got you into trouble in the first place.

Emergencies

True emergencies are different. Contact your lawyer as soon as you can, before incurring the expense if possible. The Bankruptcy Code has a procedure for obtaining trustee approval and modifying your plan to include emergency expenses.

Automobiles

Along with death and taxes, another of life's certainties is that cars die, often when you need them most. So what do you do if your car croaks while you are in the middle of a Chapter 13?

If you own the late, great car outright and don't owe anything, you can probably go out and buy a new one, assuming you have the cash. But check with your lawyer first about local rules and customs.

If you need to finance the new car, it's not that easy. You should contact your lawyer, who, with the trustee's approval, will ask the court to approve the credit transaction.

If the car that died was financed, there is another problem. The creditor who financed the car was promised certain payments under your plan. Ideally, you could try to modify your plan, give back the car, and avoid paying the balance of the loan. Some courts will allow this, whereas others will hold you to your original commitment. You'll need to consult your lawyer.

Postpetition Income Taxes

Filing Chapter 13 doesn't suspend your obligation to pay income taxes that accrue after filing your bankruptcy petition. For example, if you filed bankruptcy in July 1996, your income tax return for 1996 is not due until 1997 and any taxes owed on the filing date are deemed postpetition. In other words, you are on the hook.

Ideally, if your employer deducted enough from your paycheck, you won't owe additional taxes. However, consumers often get hit with an unexpected tax bill on April 15, and there is a temptation— since the debtor is already on a tight budget—to ignore the obligation. That's the worst thing to do. Call your lawyer instead.

The Bankruptcy Code arms the IRS with several weapons in dealing with postpetition taxes, and, to put it bluntly, you are largely subject to the whim of a tax collector. The IRS can ignore your bankruptcy and collect the taxes from you immediately, wait until your plan is completed and then collect, or simply file a proof of claim in your case.

Your lawyer will try to persuade the tax collector to choose an option that benefits both you and Uncle Sam. For instance, if the tax problem arises early on in your case and the plan provides for relatively large payments to unsecured creditors, the best course would be for the IRS to file a proof of claim immediately. That way, money for taxes comes out of the share delegated to the unsecured creditors.

Joe thought he had it made. He'd faithfully made all his Chapter 13 payments for four and one-half years and was looking forward to his completion discharge in just a few months. Then disaster struck when a tax collector thoughtlessly filed a proof of claim for postpetition income taxes that was a lot more than Joe could pay over the remaining life of the plan. The court dismissed his case, and all his good work was for naught.

In sum, the lesson here is to carefully consider the possibility of postpetition income taxes before filing for bankruptcy. And if an unexpected tax liability pops up after you file, call a lawyer immediately.

Phyllis and Tom wisely called their lawyer, who immediately filed a modified Chapter 13 plan. The plan, accepted by the court, extended the previous schedule and established payments that Phyllis and Tom could make.

12

· ·

CHECKLISTS—
DOS AND DON'TS

There's a lot to keep in mind throughout the bankruptcy process, and the aim of this book is to make the process as painless and intuitive as possible. This chapter provides a brief checklist of things you should and shouldn't do before filing and after the case is resolved.

BEFORE FILING

Collect Records

Before meeting with your lawyer, you should collect the following:

- names and addresses of all your creditors
- loan documents where a creditor may have a mortgage or security interest
- papers served on you in any lawsuit or foreclosure
- your "tax transcript" if you owe income taxes
- dates when any student loans first became due and dates of any deferments
- the exact amount you are behind on your mortgage or car loans
- the exact amount of any back alimony or child support that you owe
- copies of any divorce decree or separation agreement requiring you to pay money.

Do . . .

• Withdraw your funds from any bank where you owe money. But don't actually close the account if the bank has collateral, such as your car, or the lending institution may attempt to immediately repossess the property.

• Open new checking and savings accounts in a different bank, and deposit only the minimum amount required.

• Apply for new credit cards or charge accounts, and be scrupulously honest on any credit application.

• Continue making payments on your home and car if you intend to keep them.

• Consider paying off a small balance on a credit card or charge account so you will have credit privileges immediately. Be careful not to pay $600 or more to any single creditor, so the trustee can't get the money back as a preferential transfer (see "Preferential Transfers" in chapter 7, "Games People Play").

• File for a rapid income tax refund (if you are entitled to a refund), and spend the money on house payments, car payments, or current living expenses.

• Select a lawyer who specializes in bankruptcy, and be completely open and truthful with your attorney. Be certain to inform the lawyer of any pending civil or criminal matters. It is equally important to inform your divorce, personal injury, or criminal lawyer of your bankruptcy plans.

• Have your name removed from any will or insurance policy in which you are a beneficiary. This way, if your benefactor dies before you file, or within six months after filing, the money or property will at least go to someone other than your creditors.

• Double-check all the documents you provide your lawyer with to make sure that all your creditors are listed, their addresses correct, and that your name, address, and social security number are correct.

• Develop a monthly budget showing your income and expenses (see appendix 4).

Don't . . .

• Borrow money from friends or relatives in an attempt to pay your debts. These people will suffer a lot more if you file bankruptcy than mega credit card companies, which figure the cost of bankruptcy into their astronomical interest rates.

• Pay any debts, except those mentioned in the preceding section, without first checking with your lawyer.

• Make any gifts or transfer property in an attempt to keep these assets away from creditors.

• Ignore lawsuits.

• Give any creditor a postdated check.

• Reveal to a creditor who holds the title to your car that you are considering bankruptcy.

• Agree to pay joint debts if you are in the middle of a divorce matter. This might render some debts incurred before filing bankruptcy nondischargeable.

• Have any large checks outstanding on the petition date.

• File any past-due income tax returns if you think you owe taxes. However, have them prepared and ready to file.

• Forget to tell your lawyer about any property you own, even if you think that it's worthless.

• Make any unusual or large contributions to a pension fund.

• Make any withdrawals from your pension.

• Move out of your homestead or enter into a contract to sell it.

• Allow a foreclosure sale to occur or give a creditor a deed in lieu of foreclosure without first getting tax advice. Sometimes these actions create tax liability no one thinks about, especially when you don't get any money from them. This liability can sometimes be avoided through proper timing of your bankruptcy petition.

AFTER FILING

Do . . .

• If any lawsuits or foreclosures are pending against you, immediately inform the lawyer for the opposing party of your bankruptcy.

• If your paycheck is being garnished, tell your employer that you have filed and that any funds earned after the petition date are not subject to the garnishment.

• If you don't have health insurance that is paid up to date, contact your doctor's office, explain the situation, and ask what payment arrangements will be required for further treatment.

• Keep the court, the trustee, and your lawyer informed of your address at all times.

• Immediately review your bankruptcy documents to make sure that all your assets are listed.

• Go to your 341 meeting early, and watch other folks go through it.

• Make sure to get your first Chapter 13 payment to the trustee within thirty days of filing.

• Tell your lawyer as soon as possible if you will be unable to make your Chapter 13 payments.

• Make sure that the taxing authorities file a proof of claim in a Chapter 7 asset case where you owe nondischargeable taxes.

• Make sure that all secured creditors file a proof of claim in a Chapter 13 case.

• Check the claims register in a Chapter 13 case to make sure the claims filed by creditors are correct.

• In a Chapter 13 case where you are paying the value of your car through the plan, ask the creditor to release the title as soon as the amount specified in the plan is paid. Secured claims are typically paid before other claims, so your car might be paid off in the early stages of the plan.

• Tell your lawyer if any notice sent by the court is returned to you because the address was wrong.

• Order credit reports about six months after filing to make sure that they reflect that all your debts were included in the bankruptcy.

• Carefully read all notices from the court.

• Keep all your bankruptcy paperwork in a safe place.

Don't . . .

• Quit your job if you are entitled to termination benefits.

• Cash any checks you receive after filing and before the 341 meeting without first checking with your lawyer.

• Incur any new consumer debt without the trustee's consent in a Chapter 13.

• Move from your homestead or enter a contract to sell it without first checking with your lawyer.

• Surrender any collateral to a secured creditor before the 341 meeting.

13

. . . .

DEBT FREE
WITHOUT BANKRUPTCY

Shelly, a latter-day Thoreau, lived simply and cheaply for most of her life. Her home was a simple cabin in the woods, and she existed on a vegetarian diet. She had no interest in material possessions and was free of debt until a personal crisis led her on a three-year spending binge. Now she's got more bills than she can ever handle. Is bankruptcy the answer?

When the debt mountain is simply too steep, when the meager minimum payments fail to keep pace with exorbitant interest rates and late charges, when there is no light at the end of the tunnel, bankruptcy is clearly a solution worth considering. But it's not always the only solution or even the best solution.

There are drawbacks to bankruptcy. You may have to liquidate assets, possibly even your home, and getting a mortgage or car loan in the immediate future may not be possible. Other routes to financial freedom will, in some cases, prove to be the better alternative.

Depending on your situation, the best alternative could be to:

- sell assets to pay debts in full
- negotiate with creditors, including the IRS, with the aim of getting debts down to a manageable level
- restructure your home mortgage
- take out a home equity loan
- do nothing.

SELLING ASSETS

If you own assets that you are just going to lose in bankruptcy, and if you can sell the items off to pay your debts, that's the way to go. But most people don't have that option. Typically, people who accumulate debt buying mall junk on credit cards end up with literally no salable assets. But if you can get yourself out of financial trouble without going through bankruptcy, and can do so without unreasonable sacrifice, by all means do it.

Bankruptcy remains an alternative if you get to the point where the assets you can reasonably part with won't cover the debt. You need somewhere to live. You may well need a car. Someday you will need a pension. Bankruptcy will protect all of those things and remains the best option, unless you can eliminate your debt by selling off nonessentials.

NEGOTIATING WITH CREDITORS

Faced with the option of negotiating or litigating, many creditors are willing to bargain. With a little persistence, and reasonable expectations, you may be able to negotiate smaller payments and avoid the hassle of bankruptcy. Sometimes this works to both your advantage and the creditor's.

Workout Agreements

Traditionally, nonbankruptcy workout agreements fall into three categories:

- composition plans, where creditors all agree to accept less in full settlement of the debts
- extension plans, which merely extend the term for repayment
- a combination of both, where debts are reduced and paid over an extended time period.

The problem with these plans is that all your creditors must go along, and the more creditors you have the harder it is to get them all to agree to a payment plan. In addition, you will need a lawyer to negotiate settlement agreements, and legal fees may be prohibitive.

Workout agreements are most commonly used when a person has valuable nonexempt assets worth enough to pay his or her debts but needs some time to sell the property without having to wrestle with creditors. In consumer cases it is the rare debtor who has enough assets to pay her or his debts.

"Threatening" Bankruptcy

Some creditors might agree to settle for a pittance if convinced that you are prepared to file bankruptcy, in which case they would get nothing. When there are just a few creditors, you might be able to persuade them to settle for little more than what it costs to file bankruptcy. If you have a large number of creditors, this approach won't work, simply because it'll be too expensive for you to pay each of them a significant amount.

As we said in the section on judgment liens in chapter 9, "Home Sweet Home," it's better to settle this suit before a judgment is entered if bankruptcy is on the horizon and you intend to keep your home. Because of the uncertainty as to whether judgment liens can be avoided in their entirety or whether they hang around, it is probably preferable to file bankruptcy before such a lien is lodged.

But let's assume that someone successfully sued you for $30,000 over a bad business deal. You don't have any other debt problems, and your property consists primarily of your exempt homestead, car, and pension. If you file bankruptcy, the person who sued you is out of luck. So maybe this individual will accept $1,000 in full satisfaction. It's a good deal for the person who sued because he or she would get nothing if you filed; it's a good deal for you because you avoid the expense and hassle of bankruptcy by paying just a little more than the cost of filing.

The success of this strategy depends on your convincing the creditor that you are truly prepared to file bankruptcy. The best way to accomplish this is to hire a known bankruptcy specialist to handle the negotiation. This way, the creditor knows you're serious. Also, your chances are better if the creditor has an attorney who knows enough about bankruptcy to recognize a good deal when he or she sees one. Credit card companies will rarely agree to this; they'd rather force you into bankruptcy.

WARNING! Don't threaten a no-asset bankruptcy unless you're prepared to follow through. The 1994 amendments can be interpreted to make it a crime to intentionally mislead someone that you are going to file a bankruptcy where that person would get nothing.

Consumer Credit Counseling Service

Most communities have mediation centers that can help you devise a reasonable payment proposal. In addition, there's the Consumer Credit Counseling Service, a nonprofit group that helps people set up debt repayment plans. CCCS is an organization created and maintained by large institutional creditors for the purpose of helping consumers avoid bankruptcy.

CCCS will act as an intermediary between you and the creditors. It can often get late fees dropped and wage garnishments revoked. Typically, you and the CCCS counselor, with a lot of input from the creditor, devise a repayment schedule. Then you make regular payments to the CCCS, which forwards the money to the creditor.

Sometimes CCCS charges a fairly nominal sum, usually under $25 a month, but it often works for free. There are upward of 1,000 CCCS offices nationwide. To find one near you, call the main office at (800)388-2227, or write to the headquarters at 8611 Second Avenue, Suite 100, Silver Spring, Maryland 20910.

CCCS is most useful to you in either of the following situations:

- The total amount of your debts is small enough that you are sure you'll be able to pay, if just given enough time.
- You intend to file bankruptcy eventually but need to buy some time. For example, you may be presently ineligible for bankruptcy, or you may be waiting until student loans or taxes become dischargeable.

While organizations like CCCS offer valuable assistance, sometimes they also have some serious shortcomings; the foremost one is that they are allied with creditors and have an institutional bias against bankruptcy, even when it is in your best interest.

Some counselors are very good, and if a person's situation is truly hopeless, will immediately refer the person to a bankruptcy attorney. Others think that it's their mission in life to talk people out of filing bankruptcy. They strenuously push repayment plans, which are often doomed to failure. Additionally, they often fail to get the principal amount of your debts reduced and are not much help in extending payments on secured debts. So if you go the CCCS route, know the score before agreeing to anything.

> After suffering for years from cancer, Ron's wife died, leaving him with $76,000 in medical bills and $24,000 in other debt incurred to make her last years more comfortable. A credit counseling agency convinced Ron to sell the family home and cash in his pension. Bad advice. Even after liquidating all his assets, Ron was still $27,000 in the hole and still had creditors on his tail. He ultimately ended up in bankruptcy, but by then his home and pension, which would have been preserved had he filed for protection earlier, were long gone. The credit agency was looking out for creditors and, from Ron's standpoint, only made a bad situation that much worse.

RESTRUCTURING HOME MORTGAGES

By refinancing your mortgage—in effect, trading it in for a new one with a more favorable interest rate—you can drastically cut your monthly payment. For instance, you can easily get your payment down a couple of hundred dollars a month or more by knocking a couple of points off your mortgage interest. Be wary, however, of the variable interest mortgages, which fluctuate, usually with the prime rate. They have a nasty tendency to go up at the worst possible time.

Generally, refinancing makes economic sense only when the rates have fallen a full two percentage points. Otherwise, the closing costs and fees will devour any potential savings.

HOME EQUITY LOANS/SECOND MORTGAGES

Banks have been promoting so-called home equity loans, which essentially allow lenders to bleed all the equity out of their home. In some regards, it's a good deal: you can consolidate your debts into a mortgage and deduct the interest and closing fees from your income taxes.

However, most people who attack problem debt with this strategy end up with the short end of the stick. They've suddenly come into more money, which, unless they have Herculean self-discipline, doesn't get used for its intended purpose of reducing another loan. Also, since home equity loans usually carry a steeper interest rate than other loans, the savings—if any—is insignificant.

If you take out a loan to pay a number of smaller bills, you really don't accomplish very much. You just exchange a lot of small bills for a large one and probably pay some loan fees as well.

Another problem with home equity loans is that they create a lien on your home: most debts are dischargeable in bankruptcy, but if a debt is secured—as is a home equity loan—you must either pay it or surrender the collateral.

Not convinced? Think of it this way: If you owed $10,000 on several credit card bills, you could simply wipe out the debts in bankruptcy. On the other hand, if you consolidated the bills into a single loan secured by your home, you would still have to pay if you filed bankruptcy, unless you were willing to give up your home.

IGNORING CREDITORS

It's pretty hard to flat-out ignore creditors. Just the same, sometimes it makes perfect financial and legal sense.

If you live simply, have little income or property, plan to maintain that lifestyle in the future, and don't give a darn about your credit rating, it just might be okay to do nothing.

You can't be jailed for failure to pay debts (but you can be jailed for fraud or theft, so watch your step). Creditors can't rob you of basic necessities, like clothes and food. A good chunk of your income, as well as social security benefits, welfare, and unemployment are also off-limits.

You can be sued, of course, but even bill collectors can't take blood from a stone. If you own virtually nothing and plan to own nothing, at least for several years until the statute of limitations runs out, you may be essentially immune from lawsuits. Frequently, creditors recognize the futility of going after some people and don't even bother to sue. They eat the loss—and then claim it as a tax deduction.

Again, this maneuver may make financial sense, but it is fairly irresponsible and reckless and could have serious consequences down the road when you have a sudden, urgent need for credit. And even if you choose to ignore creditors, it's hard to forget that they are there, ready to pounce on any nonexempt asset. Collection agencies routinely monitor local savings institutions. As soon as you make a deposit, you can bet they'll be there with hands out. So take this route only with a clear and calculated understanding of what is at stake.

DEALING WITH THE IRS

Any nonbankruptcy solution to your tax problems requires IRS cooperation. Taxpayers have no right to force payment agreements on the IRS, but if an agreement is made, it cannot be arbitrarily amended or set aside.

If your only tax problem is paying the current year's tax bill, and you owe less than $10,000, the IRS will usually allow you up to three years to pay. To apply, attach IRS form 9465 (Installment Agreement Request) to your tax return and mail it in. Be aware, however, that interest and penalties continue to accrue.

In negotiating any other type of solution, you should hire an experienced lawyer or accountant to represent you. Many IRS employees in the collection system are poorly trained and, frankly, intoxicated on their own power. They know, for example, that with the push of a computer button they can seize your pay or bank account. This fosters an obnoxious arrogance and makes a few of these people extremely unpleasant to deal with (although once you retain a lawyer or accountant, these agents cannot directly contact you).

To make matters worse, many collection activities are handled by massive computerized collection centers involving Automated Collection Systems (ACS). Dealing with them is an exercise in bureaucratic futility, and you don't have to stand for it. An experienced tax practitioner knows how to get your account transferred to a local office and placed with an actual person. This is a critical first step in the negotiation process. The only way to deal with the IRS is person to person.

Collection Information Statements

If you owe more than $10,000, you'll have to complete a Collection Information Statement, or CIS, before the IRS will consider a payment plan. One of the purposes of a CIS is to present your financial situation so the IRS can determine how much you can pay. But it also serves another purpose: it identifies the location of each of your assets, making it much easier to seize them if an agreement is not reached or you fail to live up to the pact.

Amount of Payments

The IRS will normally require payments equal to all your net income less "necessary living expenses." Some collection employees have pretty bizarre notions of how much it costs to live and demand completely unrealistic payment plans. But your lawyer or accountant might be able to get this employee overruled by his or her boss.

There is not much point in agreeing to a payment structure you can't meet, especially if you completed a CIS telling the IRS where to get each of your assets.

If the CIS shows that you have any liquid assets—such as cash, stock, or bonds—equal to the amount of tax you owe, the IRS will demand immediate payment. It may also insist that you max out cash advances on your credit cards and turn over the proceeds. So long as it gets its pound of flesh, the IRS doesn't seem to care whether you run up your credit cards so high that you are forced into bankruptcy court. (Remember that under the 1994 amendments, loans to pay federal taxes are not dischargeable in Chapter 7.)

However, the courts are starting to frown on overbearing IRS behavior. In a 1995 case out of the Southern District of Georgia, the judge severely scolded the IRS, stating: "Yet again the IRS's money grubbing zeal has led it afoul. Not satisfied to wait their turn, the tax vultures swooped in early to pick up the bones of this bankruptcy carcass only to find that this one still had some fight in it. Now while the IRS hops away with its tail feathers between its legs, the taxpayer is left to pay for this egregious folly. This type of willful violation of a taxpayer's rights . . . demonstrated its lack of respect for the taxpayer. It is time the IRS paid heed to the oft quoted phrase: 'The means do not justify the ends.' "*

---

* *In re Washington,* 184 BR 172, 175 (S.D. Ga. 1995).

Conditions of an Installment Agreement

An installment agreement requires that you:

- make all payments on time
- file all future tax returns and pay the tax in full
- furnish updated financial information whenever requested
- agree that any state or federal refunds be applied to the unpaid taxes.

You also agree that the installment agreement can be modified or even terminated by the IRS if your financial picture improves.

Installment Agreements and Bankruptcy Planning

Your practitioner should be keenly aware of how an installment agreement might affect a bankruptcy down the road. He or she should consider:

- *Statute of limitations on collection.* If the term of the agreement expires less than one year before the ten-year statute of limitations, the IRS will insist that you agree to extend it for up to five years—something you should not do without careful consideration. You may well be better off putting up with the IRS for a little longer and letting the statute of limitations expire. Then you're home free.
- *Time periods for dischargeability.* An installment agreement does not extend the various time periods that must pass to render taxes dischargeable in bankruptcy.
- *Tax liens.* Taxes may be much more difficult to discharge or manage in bankruptcy if a tax lien has been filed. In some cases the IRS may postpone filing a lien as long as an installment agreement is being honored.
- *Allocating tax payments.* Ordinarily, when you make voluntary payments to the IRS, you can insist that they be applied first to the most recent year's tax. As time goes by, taxes for the earlier years will become dischargeable if you file bankruptcy. Unfortunately, you surrender this right when entering an installment agreement because you give the IRS the right to schedule the payments to maximize recovery.

Achieving "Uncollectible" Status

If the IRS determines that collecting the tax would create an "undue hardship," it may suspend collection efforts indefinitely. (In IRS-speak, the account is "53'd," based on the number of the form the revenue officer must complete when reporting an account uncollectible.)

However, the tax is not abated. Taxes and penalties continue to accrue, and tax liens are not released. And of course, the IRS will continue to take your refunds. (The ten-year statute of limitations on collection continues to run, however.) The IRS will reopen the account just before the statute is about to expire and possibly try to intimidate you into signing a waiver of the statute of limitations. Don't do it. See a tax specialist.

Undue hardship means that a taxpayer would not be able to meet necessary living expenses if required to make installment payments or if the IRS seized his or her assets. The service distinguishes between "undue hardship," and "mere inconvenience," usually finding in favor of the former when it thinks it's not worth pursuing you, and finding the latter when it might be worth its effort to go after your assets. When it puts an account in "uncollectible status," the IRS will frequently file a Notice of Tax Lien (see the tax lien section in chapter 4, "Forgive Us Our Trespasses") if one has not already been filed.

Offers in Compromise

Unlike a payment agreement, an accepted Offer in Compromise results in an actual reduction on the amount you have to pay. The IRS accepts an offer when there is doubt as to whether it can collect the full amount. If the IRS thinks you could somehow pay the taxes, it won't accept an offer, regardless of hardship.

In determining how much it will accept in settlement, the IRS looks at both the assets you now own as well as your future earning ability. The taxing authority calculates how much it would receive from a quick sale of all your assets and adds a lump sum amount based on the amount it thinks you would have been able to pay on taxes over the next five years.

An offer is made on an official IRS form that requires you to waive valuable rights including:

- the ten-year statute of limitations on collection for the period the offer was pending, plus another year, and
- the right to receive any back tax refunds or credits.

When you make the offer you'll also have to submit a CIS showing the location of each of your assets. However, the IRS usually suspends collection activity while the offer is pending.

A disadvantage of making an Offer in Compromise is that it may delay the time for filing bankruptcy. One of the conditions for discharging a tax in either Chapter 7 or Chapter 13 is that it must have been assessed more than 240 days before the bankruptcy is filed. If you submit an Offer in Compromise within 240 days after a tax is assessed, the clock stops. To discharge these taxes in bankruptcy, you'll have to wait for a time period equal to the balance of the 240 days, plus the time your offer was pending, plus 30 days.

Taxpayer Ombudsman

The taxpayer ombudsman operates under the IRS Problem Resolution Program and is supposed to be the taxpayer's advocate if a taxpayer is suffering a "significant hardship" because of the way the IRS is administering the tax laws. The ombudsman has authority to issue Taxpayer Assistance Orders, which can, at least temporarily, stop collection activities.

An application of a Taxpayer Assistance Order can be made on an official IRS form or any other signed writing addressed to the IRS Problem Resolution Office in the district where you live.

The disadvantage of a Taxpayer Assistance Order is that it suspends the statute of limitations as to any IRS activity affected by the order. Even more important, any time a Taxpayer Assistance Order is in effect does not count toward tax periods for discharging taxes.

A FINAL REMINDER:
BANKRUPTCY IS NOT ABOUT GUILT

In this chapter we have provided some information to help you decide whether bankruptcy, either now or later, is your best choice. In our view, one alternative is not morally superior to any other. It's just a matter of rationally deciding which avenue is best—that is, best for you and your family, not best for somebody else.

> Shelly decided to simply put the bad years, and bad debts, out of her mind, treat it all as a bad dream, and get on with her back-to-nature lifestyle. The creditors considered suing but decided the case wasn't worth the attorney fees. Shelly's credit rating is shot, of course, but she doesn't have any use for credit anyhow. Now her problems are out of sight, out of mind, and—in a legal sense—out of creditors' reach.

Afterword

. . . .

We hope that by now you either have broken the yoke of financial slavery or at the least can see salvation. Now the key is to remain debt free.

Bad influences abound. Consider, for instance, the federal government. If you've been half as irresponsible, reckless, and deceptive as Uncle Sam, chances are you are reading this in a prison cell! And, as you probably already know, credit card companies are eager to offer credit even to people who have been through bankruptcy. Although tempting problem debtors with credit is the moral equivalent of standing outside an Alcoholics Anonymous (AA) meeting on a hot summer day and offering cold beers to the people coming out, the credit industry is perfectly willing to lead people back to financial hell. Resisting temptation sometimes takes olympian efforts, but just by reading this book you have indicated you are ready to take control and responsibility.

Think about the price you've paid for credit in the past, and not just in terms of exorbitant interest rates. Consider the emotional carnage, the disruption, and the stress that goes with it. And think about your loss of freedom. Whenever you overextend your credit, you give someone else control over your life. Too often, the cycle of debt, and the loss of control, resume after bankruptcy.

However, there is help available and there is support, appropriately from a group modeled after Alcoholics Anonymous.

It's called Debtors Anonymous, and it was founded in 1976 by a reformed alcoholic who, twenty-seven years earlier, had given up drinking with the help of AA. Now there are more than 400 chapters.

Like AA, Debtors Anonymous encompasses a multistage process

of recognizing the signs of compulsive debt, addressing the problem, and gradually taking control. DA is a self-help group, not a self-flagellation society. Members are committed to repaying their debts in full—but only on a schedule that is realistic, and tolerable and consistent with a reasonable lifestyle. The preamble to DA's constitution, recited at the beginning of every meeting, declares that Debtors Anonymous "is a fellowship of men and women who share their experience, strength, and hope with each other that they may solve their common problem and help others to recover from compulsive debt."

For information about Debtors Anonymous, write to: DA General Services Board, P.O. Box 400, Grand Central Station, New York, NY 10163-0400.

We encourage you to explore Debtors Anonymous. But most important, we view debt relief as a journey to financial freedom, not a never-ending road to Calvary. What getting out of debt is really about is opening your life to prosperity and happiness, one day at a time. You can do it, and the rewards are immeasurable. Good luck.

Appendix 1

. . . .

FAIR DEBT COLLECTION

Georgie works for a credit collection agency and gets his kicks trying to intimidate debtors. He calls at all hours, threatens to get the debtor fired or jailed, and essentially bullies people. However, it's Georgie who may end up in trouble. Under federal law, overzealous collectors can be sued within a year of the violation—for actual damages, punitive damages up to $1,000, reasonable attorney fees, and court costs.

Many states have laws to protect you from collection bullies, but even if your state doesn't offer a shield, the federal government does. The Fair Debt Collection Practices Act (FDCPA) is a weapon on your side; it applies to professional debt collectors when they are attempting to collect consumer debts.

The major limitation of the FDCPA is that it governs only those who collect debts on behalf of others. It does not apply to the original creditor. For example, the act does not apply when the phone company is trying to collect its own bill, but if the company forwards the account to a collection agency, that agency is subject to the act.

Unfortunately, the FDCPA doesn't apply to the IRS or other taxing authorities. But it does apply to attorneys who regularly collect consumer debts.

The FDCPA comprises sections 801 through 817 of the federal Consumer Credit Protection Act. Sometimes it's referred to as 15 USC § 1692, which is its location in the U.S. Code.

When Congress enacted the FDCPA in 1977, it stated its attitude in no uncertain terms in section 802(a): "There is abundant evidence of the use of abusive, deceptive, and unfair debt collection practices by many debt collectors. Abusive debt collection practices contribute to the number of personal bankruptcies, to marital instability, to the loss of jobs, and to invasions of individual privacy."

The act specifies when, where, and how a professional debt collector may contact you concerning a consumer debt. It also outlaws certain dirty tricks used by bill collectors in the past. And finally, it restricts communications with third persons concerning your debt.

Although the provisions of the Fair Debt Collection Practices Act have been addressed earlier, this appendix lays out the specifics of the law to show you exactly where you stand. Then, when the bill collector calls, you can cite the law to him or her—chapter and verse.

WHEN DEBT COLLECTORS CAN CONTACT YOU

Debt collectors cannot contact you at any time that they have reason to believe is inconvenient. And for the most part, they can't contact you at all if you've notified them in writing to lay off.

Section 805(a) Says:

Without the prior consent of the consumer given directly to the debt collector or the express permission of a court of competent jurisdiction, a debt collector may not communicate with a consumer in connection with the collection of any debt—

(1) at any unusual time or place or at a time or place known or which should be known to be inconvenient to the consumer. In the absence of knowledge of circumstances to the contrary, a debt collector shall assume that the convenient time for communicating with a consumer is after 8 o'clock antemeridian and before 9 o'clock postmeridian, local time at the consumer's location;

(2) if the debt collector knows the consumer is represented by an attorney with respect to such debt and has knowledge of, or can readily ascertain, such attorney's name and address, unless the attorney fails to respond within a reasonable period of time to a communication from the debt collector or unless the attorney consents to direct communication with the consumer.

Section 805(c) Says:

If a consumer notifies a debt collector in writing that the consumer refuses to pay a debt or that the consumer wishes the debt collector to cease further communication with the consumer, the debt collector shall not communicate further with the consumer with respect to such debt, except—

(1) to advise the consumer that the debt collector's further efforts are being terminated;

(2) to notify the consumer that the debt collector or creditor may invoke specified remedies which are ordinarily invoked by such debt collector or creditor; or

(3) where applicable, to notify the consumer that the debt collector or creditor intends to invoke a specified remedy. If such notice from the consumer is made by mail, notification shall be complete upon receipt.

Section 805(d) Says:

For the purpose of this section, the term "consumer" includes the consumer's spouse, parent (if the consumer is a minor), guardian, executor or administrator.

WHERE DEBT COLLECTORS CAN CONTACT YOU

Debt collectors may not contact you at any place that could be inconvenient for you or cause you unnecessary embarrassment. See section 805(a)(1), above. Also, they may not contact you at work if they have been informed that your employer forbids such communication.

Section 805(a) Says:

Without the prior consent of the consumer given directly to the debt collector or the express permission of a court of competent jurisdiction, a debt collector may not communicate with a consumer in connection with the collection of any debt—

(3) at the consumer's place of employment if the debt collector knows or has reason to know that the consumer's employer prohibits the consumer from receiving such communication.

HARASSMENT AND INTIMIDATION ARE FORBIDDEN

The FDCPA forbids debt collectors from engaging in any conduct that would tend to harass, oppress, or abuse you. For instance, they can't unnecessarily leave messages with a third person for you to return a call from the debt collector; contact you too frequently; imply the use of force against you; use foul language; or threaten to embarrass you.

Section 806 Says:

A debt collector may not engage in any conduct the natural consequence of which is to harass, oppress, or abuse any person in connection with the collection of a debt. Without limiting the general application of the foregoing, the following conduct is a violation of this section:

(1) the use or threat of use of violence or other criminal means to harm the physical person, reputation, or property of any person.

(2) the use of obscene or profane language or language the natural consequence of which is to abuse the hearer or reader.

(3) the publication of a list of consumers who allegedly refuse to pay debts, except to a consumer reporting agency or to [persons having a legitimate business interest in this information].

(4) the advertisement for sale of any debt to coerce payment of the debt.

(5) causing a telephone to ring or engaging any person in telephone conversation repeatedly or continuously with intent to annoy, abuse, or harass any person at the called number.

(6) except as provided in section 804, the placement of telephone calls without meaningful disclosure of the caller's identity.

DIRTY TRICKS ARE OUTLAWED

The FDCPA prohibits false, misleading, or unfair practices by debt collectors, including a number of specific practices that creditors have traditionally used to collect debts. These provisions are especially interesting because they point out tactics that creditors who are not subject to the act may still use against you, unless your state has its own law forbidding these tricks.

Section 807 Says:

A debt collector may not use any false, deceptive, or misleading representations or means in connection with the collection of any debt. Without limiting the general application of the foregoing, the following is a violation of this section:

(1) the false representation or implication that the debt collector is vouched for, bonded by, or affiliated with the United States or any State, including the use of any badge, uniform, or facsimile thereof.

(2) the false representation of—

(A) the character, amount, or legal status of any debt; or

(B) any services rendered or compensation which may be lawfully received by any debt collector for the collection of a debt.

(3) the false representation or implication that any individual is an attorney or that any communication is from an attorney.

(4) the representation or implication that nonpayment of any debt will result in the arrest or imprisonment of any person or the seizure, garnishment, attachment, or sale of any property or wages of any person unless such action is lawful and the debt collector or creditor intends to take such action.

(5) the threat to take any action that cannot legally be taken or that is not intended to be taken.

(6) the false representation or implication that a sale, referral, or other transfer of any interest in a debt shall cause the consumer to—

(A) lose any claim or defense to payment of the debt; or

(B) become subject to any practice prohibited by this [act].

(7) the false representation or implication that the consumer

committed any crime or other conduct in order to disgrace the consumer.

(8) Communicating or threatening to communicate to any person credit information which is known or which should be known to be false, including the failure to communicate that a disputed debt is disputed.

(9) The use or distribution of any written communication which simulates or is falsely represented to be a document authorized, issued, or approved by any court, official, or agency of the United States or any State, or which creates a false impression as to its source, authorization, or approval.

(10) The use of any false representation or deceptive means to collect or attempt to collect any debt or to obtain information concerning a consumer.

(11) Except as otherwise provided for [under section 804, which allows inquiries to determine a debtor's whereabouts; section 804 is discussed in more detail later in this appendix] the failure to disclose clearly in all communications made to collect a debt or to obtain information about a consumer, that the debt collector is attempting to collect a debt and that any information obtained will be used for that purpose.

(12) the false representation or implication that accounts have been turned over to innocent purchasers for value.

(13) the false representation or implication that documents are legal process.

(14) the use of any business, company, or organization name other than the true name of the debt collector's business, company, or organization.

(15) the false representation or implication that documents are not legal process forms or do not require action by the consumer.

(16) the false representation or implication that a debt collector operates or is employed by a consumer reporting agency as defined [in the Fair Credit Reporting Act].

Section 808 Says:

A debt collector may not use unfair or unconscionable means to collect or attempt to collect any debt. Without limiting the general application of the foregoing, the following conduct is a violation of this section:

(1) the collection of any amount (including any interest, fee, charge, or expense incidental to the principal obligation) unless such amount is expressly authorized by the agreement creating the debt or permitted by law.

(2) the acceptance by a debt collector from any person of a check or other payment instrument postdated by more than five days unless such person is notified in writing of the debt collector's intent to deposit such check or instrument not more than ten nor less than three business days prior to such deposit.

(3) the solicitation by a debt collector of any postdated check or other postdated payment instrument for the purpose of threatening or instituting criminal prosecution.

(4) depositing or threatening to deposit any postdated check or other postdated payment instrument prior to the date on such check or instrument.

(5) causing charges to be made to any person for communication by concealment of the true purpose of the communication. Such charges include, but are not limited to, collect telephone calls and telegram fees.

(6) taking or threatening to take any nonjudicial action to effect dispossession or disablement of property if—

(A) there is no present right to possession of the property claim as collateral through an enforceable security interest; or

(B) there is no present intention to take possession or disablement; or

(C) the property is exempt by law from such dispossession or disablement.

(7) communicating with a consumer regarding a debt by post card.

(8) using any language or symbol, other than the debt collector's address, on any envelope when communicating with a consumer by use of the mails or by telegram, except that a debt collector may use his business name if such name does not indicate that he is in the debt collection business.

WHEN DEBT COLLECTORS MAY CONTACT
OTHERS ABOUT YOUR DEBT

As a general rule, the FDCPA forbids debt collectors from contacting third persons about your debt, thus outlawing the common tactic of trying to shame you into paying a bill. The act contains limited exceptions allowing debt collectors to contact others in order to locate you or enforce a judgment, but it places strict limits on the practice.

Section 805(b) Says:

Except as provided in Section 804, without the prior consent of the consumer given directly to the debt collector, or the express permission of a court of competent jurisdiction, or as reasonably necessary to effectuate a postjudgment judicial remedy, a debt collector may not communicate, in connection with the collection of any debt, with any person other than the consumer, his attorney, a consumer reporting agency if otherwise permitted by law, the creditor, the attorney of the creditor, or the attorney for the debt collector.

Section 804 Says:

Any debt collector communicating with any person other than the consumer for the purpose of acquiring location information about a consumer shall—

(1) identify himself, state that he is confirming or correcting location information concerning the consumer, and, only if expressly requested, identify his employer;

(2) not state that such consumer owes any debt;

(3) not communicate with any such person more than once unless requested to do so by such person or unless the debt collector reasonably believes that the earlier response of such person is erroneous or incomplete and that such person now has correct or complete location information;

(4) not communicate by post card;

(5) not use any language or symbol on any envelope or in the contents of any communication effected by the mails or telegram that in-

dicates that the debt collector is in the debt collection business or that the communication relates to the collection of a debt; and

(6) after the debt collector knows the consumer is represented by an attorney with regard to the subject debt and has knowledge of, or can readily ascertain, such attorney's name and address, not communicate with any person other than that attorney, unless the attorney fails to respond within a reasonable period of time to communication from the debt collector.

YOUR REMEDIES

You can sue a debt collector for violating the FDCPA and recover actual damages, punitive damages up to $1,000, and attorney fees. But you must file suit within one year of the violation.

Section 813(a) Says:

Except as otherwise provided by this section, any debt collector who fails to comply with any provision of this title with respect to any person is liable to such person in an amount equal to the sum of—

(1) any actual damages sustained by such person as a result of such failure;

(2)(A) in the case of any action by an individual, such additional damages as the court may allow, but not exceeding $1,000;

(3) in the case of any successful action to enforce the foregoing liability, the costs of the action, together with a reasonable attorney's fee as determined by the court. On a finding by the court that an action under this section was brought in bad faith and for the purpose of harassment, the court may award to the defendant attorney's fees reasonable in relation to the work expended and costs.

Section 813(d) Says:

An action to enforce any liability created by this title may be brought in any appropriate United States district court without regard to the amount in controversy, or in any other court of competent jurisdiction, within one year from the date on which the violation occurs.

Appendix 2

· ·

TABLES

TABLE 1

Eligibility—Chapter 7 vs. Chapter 13

	CHAP. 7	CHAP. 13
Previous Chap. 7 or Chap. 13 discharge in case filed within six years	Not eligible for Chap. 7 discharge.[a]	Does not affect eligibility.
Debt requirements	No maximum debt limit. Possible minimum debt requirement if "substantial abuse"[b] factors present.	Maximum secured debt limit of $750,000 and unsecured debt limit of $250,000. No minimum debt requirement.
Income requirements	No maximum income limitation, unless income is so high that "substantial abuse" factors are present. No minimum income requirement.	No maximum income limitation, but high income may require higher plan payments. Minimum income necessary to make payments required by the plan.
"Good faith" limitations	"Good faith" is seldom an issue unless "substantial abuse" factors are present.	"Good faith" is required.
Effect of nondischargeable taxes, alimony, or child support	Do not affect eligibility to wipe out other debts.	Potential to indirectly affect eligibility because plan must provide that these obligations be paid in full over a period no longer than five years.

a. Unless the discharge was a Chap. 13 discharge and creditors in that case were paid at least 70 percent.

b. The concept of *substantial abuse* kicks in when your income is sufficient, after payment of all expenses, to pay all or most of your debts over the life of a Chap. 13 plan.

TABLE 2

Dischargeable Debts—Chapter 7 vs. Chapter 13

	CHAP. 7	CHAP. 13
Student loans	Discharged *only* if more than seven years old or "undue hardship" can be proved.	Same as Chap. 7.
Injuries from drunk driving	Not discharged.	Same as Chap. 7.
Criminal restitution	If imposed by a federal court, not discharged. Otherwise, discharged if the wrongful conduct occurred more than three years before the petition date.[a]	Not discharged.
Alimony and child support	Not discharged.	Not discharged, and must be paid in full over the life of plan.
Divorce obligations that are not alimony or child support	Not discharged unless unreasonably burdensome.	Discharged, unless secured.
Fines[b]	Discharged if offending conduct occurred more than three years before petition date.[c]	Not discharged.
Fraud	Not discharged.	Discharged.
Damages from intentional wrongs	Not discharged.	Discharged.
Loans obtained to pay federal income tax	Not discharged.	Discharged.
Taxes[d]	Generally not discharged.	Although generally not discharged, may usually be paid over the life of the plan, frequently without further interest or penalty.

a. Failure to make restitution payments may result in incarceration.

b. Fines imposed by a federal court as part of a criminal sentence are in a class by themselves. They follow you for twenty years, are a lien against all your property, and can't be discharged in any type of bankruptcy.

c. Discharge is not the whole story. State courts might try to put you in jail for not paying a fine.

d. See table 4 for information on discharging federal income taxes.

TABLE 3

Saving Your Home—Chapter 7 vs. Chapter 13

	CHAP. 7	CHAP. 13
Mortgage payments current, equity within the exemption	Home should not be affected. Regular payments continue.	Home should not be affected. Regular payments should continue, outside the plan if possible to avoid trustee's commission.ᵃ
Mortgage payments behind, equity within the exemption	The trustee will not assert an interest, but you will have to make up all the back payments immediately.	Must resume regular monthly payments and make up back payments over the life of the plan.ᵇ
Equity greater than exemption	Trustee can sell your home, pay you the amount of the exemption, and pay the rest to your creditors.	Trustee cannot sell your home. However, plan payments will be higher to cover the amount of your nonexempt equity over the life of the plan.
No equity, mortgages more than the property is worth	Temporarily stops foreclosure. Chap. 7 won't save home, but it will extinguish the loan.	If mortgages don't qualify for special protection given residential mortgages, bifurcation is an option.ᶜ

a. If you owe more than the property is worth, always consider whether bifurcation is an option. Despite the rule against modifying residential mortgages, many courts have allowed bifurcation in cases where the creditor has other collateral in addition to your home.

b. The Bankruptcy Code requires that back payments on residential mortgages be brought current within a "reasonable time" under the Chap. 13 plan. Some courts have said that back payments must be brought current in the early stages of the plan, but most say that they can be stretched over the full three to five years of the plan.

c. This is permitted when the mortgage holder has some other security (such as your car) or the property is other than a single-family residence.

TABLE 4

Dischargeability of Federal Income Taxes[a]

	CHAP. 7	CHAP. 13
Taxes less than three years old[b] (no IRS Notice of Tax Lien)	Not discharged. Must make payment arrangements with IRS after your bankruptcy is closed.	Not discharged, *unless* the IRS fails to file a proof of claim. But the taxes can be paid over the life of the plan without further penalties, and without postpetition interest (unless a Notice of Tax Lien has been filed; see below).
Taxes more than three years old (returns late, and within two years of the petition date; no IRS Notice of Tax Lien)[c]	Not discharged.	Discharged *unless* the taxes are assessed within 240 days of the petition date.[d]
Taxes more than three years old (return never filed; no IRS Notice of Tax Lien)	Not discharged.	Discharged *unless* the IRS filed the return for you and assessed the tax within 240 days of the petition date.
Taxes more than three years old (fraudulent taxes filed or other intentional tax evasion; no IRS Notice of Tax Lien)[e]	Not discharged.	Discharged, *unless* the IRS can convince the court to dismiss your case for "bad faith."
IRS Notice of Tax Lien filed	Even if the taxes are discharged, any property owned on the petition date, including exempt property, remains subject to the tax lien. If the taxes are discharged, any property acquired after the petition date would not be subject to the lien.	*Regardless* of whether the taxes are discharged, a Notice of Tax Lien gives the IRS a secured claim up to the value of all your property on the petition date. The secured claim must be paid, with interest, over the life of the plan.[f]
Prepetition interest	Discharged *only* if the underlying taxes are discharged.	Discharged *only* if the underlying taxes are discharged.

	CHAP. 7	CHAP. 13
Postpetition interest on prepetition taxes	Continues to accrue on nondischargeable taxes.	Does not accrue, even though the taxes are not dischargeable, *unless* a Notice of Tax Lien has been filed. If the Chap. 13 case is dismissed or converted, interest that would have accrued is revived.
Prepetition penalties	Discharged if *either* the underlying tax is discharged, or the event giving rise to the penalty occurred more than three years before the petition date.	Discharged. It makes no difference whether the prepetition taxes, to which the penalties relate, are discharged. But if a Notice of Tax Lien has been filed, the penalties are included in the amount of the government's secured claim.
Postpetition penalties on prepetition taxes	Not assessed *if* the tax is discharged. Not assessed while the case is open (usually about four months).	*Possibly*, but not definitely, assessed if the case is dismissed. Not assessed if the plan is completed.

a. If taxes are ten years old, measured from the date of assessment, they might be barred by the statute of limitations. If so, the taxes, and any associated liens, are eliminated even without filing bankruptcy.

b. Measured from the date the return was due. Usually, this is April 15 of the following year, unless the taxpayer got an extension to file. If the taxpayer had a prior bankruptcy, the time period during which the automatic stay was in effect does not count, and six months is added to the three years. Also, any period when a Taxpayer Assistance Order was in effect does not count.

c. If the taxpayer had a prior bankruptcy, the time period during which the automatic stay was in effect does not count, and six months are added to the two years. Also, any period when a Taxpayer Assistance Order was in effect does not count.

d. This 240-day period is extended by a prior bankruptcy, or Taxpayer Assistance Order, in the same way that the three-year period is extended. (See above.) In addition, any period during which an IRS Offer in Compromise was pending, plus 30 days, is added to the 240-day period. Taxes are usually assessed shortly after the return is filed. Taxes assessed later are usually those arising from an audit.

e. The IRS will sometimes make a public example of tax protestors. In a Chap. 7 the IRS will claim that the tax should not be discharged because the protestor willfully tried to evade the debt; in a Chap. 13 the IRS will argue that any attempt by a tax protestor to discharge taxes constitutes "bad faith" and, consequently, the bankruptcy petition should be rejected.

f. Instead of paying the lien for taxes that would otherwise be dischargeable, your Chap. 13 plan could propose to surrender everything you owned on the petition date to the IRS, in full satisfaction of the lien. If all you owned were household goods and a car, it is unlikely that the IRS would actually bother taking the items.

WHEN A CHAPTER 13 GOES BAD

It's unfortunate, but many Chapter 13s fail and get dismissed or converted to Chapter 7. By far the most common reason is that the debtor doesn't keep up with his or her payments. In chapter 11, "You Blew It Again?" we discussed the various options. This table illustrates the consequences of the various choices.

One of the options is to "stick with current plan." If you're having trouble making payments, the court may allow you to suspend a few payments until you get back on your feet. It also may be possible to modify your existing plan. Chapter 11 addresses these topics in detail.

TABLE 5

Impact of Various Options

	STICK WITH A CURRENT PLANᵃ	CONVERT TO CHAP. 7	DISMISS CHAP. 13/FILE NEW CHAP. 7	REQUEST HARDSHIP DISCHARGE IN EXISTING CHAP. 13
Debts incurred after petition date for present Chap. 13	Not discharged.	Discharged.	Can be included in new Chap. 7.	Not discharged.
Discharge received in a bankruptcy filed within six years of present Chap. 13	Discharge available despite the earlier bankruptcy.	Discharge unavailable *unless* the first case was a Chap. 13 and creditors in that case received at least 70 percent of their claims.	Discharge unavailable. Chap. 7 petition must be filed at least six years after first filing in order to get a discharge in the new case.	Discharge available despite the earlier bankruptcy.

	STICK WITH A CURRENT PLANᵃ	CONVERT TO CHAP. 7	DISMISS CHAP. 13/FILE NEW CHAP. 7	REQUEST HARDSHIP DISCHARGE IN EXISTING CHAP. 13
Student loans[b]	Discharged *if* more than seven years old when Chap. 13 petition was filed.	Same as sticking with the current plan.	Won't be discharged in the new Chap. 7 unless loans are seven years old when the new case is filed.[c]	Same as sticking with the current plan.
Criminal restitution sentences[d]	Not discharged.	*State* restitution not discharged unless offending conduct occurred more than three years before Chap. 13 filed. *Federal* restitution not discharged regardless of when offending conduct occurred.[e]	*State* restitution not discharged unless offending conduct occurred more than three years before new Chap. 7 filed. *Federal* restitution not discharged regardless of when offending conduct occurred.	Same as conversion to Chap. 7.
Personal injuries caused by drunk driving	Not discharged.	Not discharged.	Not discharged.	Not discharged.
Fines[f] (Chap. 13 filed before Oct. 22 1994)	Discharged.	Discharged if offending conduct occurred more than three years before Chap. 13 was filed.	Discharged if offending conduct occurred more then three years before new Chap. 7 filed.	Same as conversion to Chap. 7.
Fines[g] (Chap. 13 filed on or	Not discharged.	Discharged if offending	Discharged if offending	Same as conversion to

	STICK WITH A CURRENT PLANᵃ	CONVERT TO CHAP. 7	DISMISS CHAP. 13/FILE NEW CHAP. 7	REQUEST HARDSHIP DISCHARGE IN EXISTING CHAP. 13
after Oct. 22, 1994)		conduct occurred more than three years before Chap. 13 filed.	conduct occurred more than three years before new Chap. 7 filed.	Chap. 7.
Secured claim is being "crammed down" (value of collateral is being paid over the life of the plan)ʰ	Collateral *should* be released as soon as the cramdown amount is paid in full.	Collateral can be redeemed by paying a lump sum equal to the unpaid cramdown amount.ⁱ	Collateral will be revalued as of the date of the new Chap. 7. To redeem, debtor must pay the value of the collateral in a lump sum, with no credit given for cramdown payments made during Chap. 13 case.	Same as conversion to Chap. 7.
Property acquired after original Chap. 13 petition (cases filed before Oct. 22, 1994)	Not affected *unless* trustee or a creditor gets the court to modify the plan prior to completion of payments.	Goes to Chap. 7 trustee if not exempt at the time of conversion.	Goes to Chap. 7 trustee if not exempt at the time the new Chap. 7 is filed.	Not affected.
Property acquired after original Chap. 13 petition (cases filed on or after Oct. 22, 1994)	Not affected *unless* trustee or a creditor gets the court to modify the plan prior to completion of payments.	Does *not* go to Chap. 7 trustee unless conversion is in "bad faith."	Goes to Chap. 7 trustee if not exempt at the time the new Chap. 7 is filed.	Same as sticking with current plan.
Status of property	*Probably* no effect, but	Status of property	Exempt status determined as	*Probably* no effect, but

	STICK WITH A CURRENT PLAN[a]	CONVERT TO CHAP. 7	DISMISS CHAP. 13/FILE NEW CHAP. 7	REQUEST HARDSHIP DISCHARGE IN EXISTING CHAP. 13
changes during Chap. 13[j]	check with lawyer first.	reexamined. If it doesn't qualify as exempt on date of conversion, it goes to trustee.	of the date new Chap. 7 filed.	check with lawyer first.
Increases in value of exempt property over the exempt amount[k] (cases filed before Oct. 22, 1994)	Not affected *unless* trustee or a creditor gets the court to modify the plan prior to completion of payments.	Chap. 7 trustee will claim nonexempt equity.	Chap. 7 trustee will claim nonexempt equity.	Same as sticking with current plan.
Increases in value of exempt property over the exempt amount[l] (cases filed on or after Oct. 22, 1994)	Not affected *unless* trustee or a creditor gets the court to modify the plan prior to completion of payments.	Increased equity will *not* go to Chap. 7 trustee unless conversion is in "bad faith."	Chap. 7 trustee will claim nonexempt equity.	Not affected.
Loan is being "bifurcated" under the plan[m]	Loan term is permanently reduced if current plan is completed.	Loan term reverts to its original length.[n]	Loan term cannot be reduced.	Courts disagree on whether the loan term remains shortened.

a. Or a modified version approved by the court.

b. If debtor can show that repayment of the student loan would constitute an "undue hardship," all or a part of the loan is dischargeable, no matter how old it is.

c. Most courts would say that the time spent in Chap. 13 doesn't count toward the seven years.

d. Note: Bankruptcy discharge of restitution may not end the matter since a state could attempt to re-sentence and incarcerate the defendant if the sum is not paid.

e. If Chap. 13 case was filed on or before Sept. 13, 1994, a restitution sentence imposed by *either* a state or federal court is discharged if the offending conduct occurred more then three years before the Chap. 13 case was filed.

f. Fines imposed by a federal court as part of a criminal sentence are in a class by themselves. They follow you for twenty years, are a lien against all your property, and can't be discharged in any type of bankruptcy.

g. Fines imposed by a federal court as part of a criminal sentence are in a class by themselves. They follow you for twenty years, are a lien against all your property, and can't be discharged in any type of bankruptcy.

h. For example, if a car was worth $2,000, and the debt was $5,000, the "cram-down" amount would be $2,000.

i. In the example of footnote h., if debtor had paid $1,200 during the Chap. 13, he or she could redeem the car by paying the creditor only $800.

j. Example: Debtor moves out of property that qualified as a homestead when Chap. 13 was filed, and it becomes unqualified as a homestead because debtor rents it out *after* the Chap. 13 is filed.

k. Example: When the Chap. 13 filed, debtor had equity of $15,000 in homestead and the allowable exemption was $17,000. After the Chap. 13 was filed, debtor's equity increased to $20,000, either because the overall value of the property increased, or because the mortgage balance had been reduced.

l. Example: When the Chap. 13 filed, debtor had equity of $15,000 in homestead and the allowable exemption was $17,000. After the Chap. 13 was filed, debtor's equity increased to $20,000, either because the overall value of the property increased, or because the mortgage balance had been reduced.

m. A nonresidential loan may be "bifurcated" in Chap. 13 if the balance owed on the loan is more than the property is worth. When a loan is bifurcated the outstanding loan balance is reduced to the value of the property. The amount of loan payments remains the same, but the loan is paid off earlier. Unlike other types of loans, residential mortgages can't be modified by a Chap. 13 plan, but prior to June 1, 1993, the date of the U.S. Supreme Court decision in *Nobleman v. American Savings Bank*, 113 S.Ct. 2106 (1993), bifurcation of residential mortgages was allowed. Since bifurcation of home mortgages is no longer allowed, every effort should be made to keep a Chap. 13 filed before June 1, 1993 alive and to complete it.

n. Some courts might hold that the term remains shortened if the Chap. 13 was filed before January 15, 1992, the date of the U.S. Supreme Court decision in *Dewsnup v. Timm*, 112 S.Ct. 773 (1992). In that case, the court held that residential mortgages could not be bifurcated in Chap. 7.

Appendix 3

. . . .

EXEMPTION LAWS

FEDERAL VS. STATE EXEMPTIONS

Although bankruptcy law is generally the province of the federal government, a number of states have their own provisions with regard to exemptions, giving people the chance to choose between exemptions offered under the Bankruptcy Code and those provided by their own legislature.

Debtors can choose either local or Bankruptcy Code exemptions, based on the jurisdiction where they lived for the longest period during a 180-day span immediately preceding the petition date, in the following places: Alaska, Arkansas, Connecticut, District of Columbia, Hawaii, Massachusetts, Michigan, Minnesota, New Jersey, New Mexico, Pennsylvania, Puerto Rico, Rhode Island, South Carolina, Texas, Vermont, Virgin Islands, Washington, and Wisconsin.

Generally, you've got to stick with one set of exemptions; the law usually will not allow debtors to shop for the best of both worlds. Also, joint debtors must both agree to choose state (or, if applicable, the District of Columbia, Puerto Rico, or the Virgin Islands) exemptions. In other words, one spouse can't pluck the state exemptions if the other elects to go the federal route.

There are some federal exemptions in statutes other than those in the Bankruptcy Code, and these can be claimed in addition to state or federal bankruptcy exemptions. They include:

- veterans' benefits and military pensions
- railroad retirement payments
- social security benefits

- longshoremen's and harbor workers' death and disability benefits
- seamen's wages
- special pensions awarded to Congressional Medal of Honor winners.

The Bankruptcy Code, like state laws, comes with a smorgasbord of exemptions, including: personal injury claims and workers' compensation claims, support payments due to a debtor, and interests in certain types of insurance policies.

Most private pensions are covered by ERISA, the federal Employee Retirement Security Act of 1974. These pensions are protected even if there is no exemption because they do not become property of the estate.

You have to rely on an exemption only if your pension is not covered by ERISA, a problem that crops up with IRAs, public employee pensions, and pensions that primarily benefit only the owner of the business. These are protected only to the extent that there is an applicable federal or state exemption.

What follows is a list of many—but not all—of the commonly available exemptions. It's intended to give you a general idea of the major exemptions and an opportunity to personalize the examples sprinkled throughout this book.

BANKRUPTCY CODE EXEMPTIONS

The exemptions listed in the Bankruptcy Code are available only if the debtor lives in certain jurisdictions (check for your particular area; see below). But as we said, not all federal exemptions are found in the Bankruptcy Code; instead, they are sprinkled throughout the whole U.S. Code. And these non–Bankruptcy Code exemptions are available in all states.

The most important Bankruptcy Code exemptions cover six categories:

- Homestead: $15,000, $30,000 for joint debtors
- Household furnishings: $8,000, except for any item worth more than $400
- Tools of trade: $1,500

- Motor vehicle: $2,400
- Wages: 75 percent of weekly disposable income or thirty times the federal weekly minimum hourly wage, whichever is greater
- Retirement plans: to the extent reasonably necessary for the support of the debtor and any dependent of the debtor

Alabama

Exemptions under the Bankruptcy Code are not available.

- Homestead: $5,000 and not exceeding 160 acres in area
- Personal property: $3,000
- Wages: 75 percent exempt
- Retirement plans: public employee pensions

Alaska

Debtor can choose between state and federal exemptions.

- Homestead: $54,000
- Household goods: $3,000
- Tools of trade: $2,800
- Motor vehicle: $3,000
- Wages: weekly net earnings up to $350
- Retirement plans: IRAs

Arizona

Exemptions under the Bankruptcy Code are not available.

- Homestead: $100,000
- Household goods: $4,000
- Tools of trade: $2,500
- Motor vehicle: $1,500
- Wages: 75 percent of weekly disposable income
- Retirement plans

Arkansas

Debtor can choose between state and federal exemptions.

- Homestead: $3,300, $3,750 if married
- Household goods: $200, $500 if married or head of household
- Tools of trade: $750
- Motor vehicle: $1,250
- Wages: amount equal to sixty days' pay
- Retirement plans

California

Debtor may not choose between the exemptions in the Bankruptcy Code and those under state law, but there are two alternative sets of exemptions. One is quite similar to the exemptions under the U.S. Code. The following list of exemptions includes some of those available if the debtor does not select the set of exemptions that are similar to the Bankruptcy Code exemptions.

- Homestead: $50,000, $75,000 if debtor is a member of a family unit, $100,000 if debtor is older than sixty-five, is disabled, or has income less than $15,000
- Household goods: to the extent reasonably necessary to the debtor and dependents
- Tools of trade: $5,000
- Motor vehicle: $1,900
- Wages: 75 percent
- Retirement plans

Colorado

Exemptions under the Bankruptcy Code are not available.

- Homestead: $30,000
- Household goods: $1,500
- Tools of trade: $1,500
- Motor vehicle: $1,000
- Wages: 75 percent of weekly disposable earnings
- Retirement plans

Connecticut

Debtor can choose between state and federal exemptions.

- Homestead: $75,000
- Household goods: to the extent necessary
- Tools of trade: to the extent necessary
- Motor vehicle: $1,500
- Wages: 75 percent of weekly disposable earnings or forty times the federal minimum wage, whichever is greater
- Retirement plans

Delaware

Exemptions under the Bankruptcy Code are not available.

- Personal property: $5,000
- Wages: 85 percent
- Retirement plans: public employee pensions

District of Columbia

Debtor can choose between these and federal exemptions.

- Household goods: $300
- Tools of trade: $200
- Motor vehicle: $500, but only if used in trade or business
- Wages: 75 percent of weekly disposable wages or thirty times the weekly federal minimum hourly wage, whichever is greater
- Retirement plans: for judges or teachers, other retirement plans up to $200 per month

Florida

Exemptions under the Bankruptcy Code are not available.

- Homestead: unlimited in amount and up to 160 acres of rural land or one-half acre of city property
- Personal property: $1,000

- Wages: all disposable earnings of a head of household, otherwise 75 percent of weekly disposable wages or thirty times the weekly federal minimum hourly wage, whichever is greater
- Retirement plans

Georgia

Exemptions under the Bankruptcy Code are not available.

- Homestead: $5,000
- Household goods: $3,500, except for any item worth more than $200
- Tools of trade: $500
- Motor vehicle: $1,000
- Wages: 75 percent of weekly disposable wages or thirty times the weekly federal minimum hourly wage, whichever is greater
- Retirement plans

Hawaii

Debtor can choose between state and federal exemptions.

- Homestead: $30,000 for head of household or individual sixty-five years of age or older, $20,000 for all others
- Household goods: to the extent necessary for the debtor and his/her family
- Tools of trade: unlimited
- Motor vehicle: $1,000
- Wages: all wages for past thirty-one days exempt
- Retirement plans

Idaho

Exemptions under the Bankruptcy Code are not available.

- Homestead: $50,000
- Household goods: $4,000, except for items worth more than $500
- Tools of trade: $1,000

- Motor vehicle: $1,500
- Wages: 75 percent of weekly disposable wages or thirty times the weekly federal minimum hourly wage, whichever is greater
- Retirement plans

Illinois

Exemptions under the Bankruptcy Code are not available.

- Homestead: $7,500
- Personal property: $2,000
- Tools of trade: $750
- Motor vehicle: $1,200
- Wages: 85 percent of weekly disposable wages or forty-five times the weekly federal minimum hourly wage, whichever is greater
- Retirement plans

Indiana

Exemptions under the Bankruptcy Code are not available.

- Homestead: $7,500
- Personal property: up to $4,000
- Wages: 75 percent of weekly disposable wages or thirty times the weekly federal minimum hourly wage, whichever is greater
- Retirement plans

Iowa

Exemptions under the Bankruptcy Code are not available.

- Homestead: unlimited in amount, up to forty rural acres or one-half acre in city
- Household goods: $2,000
- Tools of trade: $10,000
- Motor vehicle: $5,000
- Wages: at least 90 percent exempt
- Retirement plans: to the extent reasonably necessary for support of debtor or dependents

Kansas

Exemptions under the Bankruptcy Code are not available.

- Homestead: unlimited in amount, up to 160 acres of farming land or one acre within city
- Household goods: to the extent reasonably necessary
- Motor vehicle: $20,000
- Wages: 75 percent of weekly disposable wages or thirty times the weekly federal minimum hourly wage, whichever is greater
- Retirement plans

Kentucky

Exemptions under the Bankruptcy Code are not available.

- Homestead: $5,000
- Household goods: $3,000
- Tools of trade: $300
- Motor vehicle: $2,500
- Wages: 75 percent of weekly disposable wages or thirty times the weekly federal minimum hourly wage, whichever is greater
- Retirement plans: public employee pensions, other pensions exempt to the extent reasonably necessary for support of debtor and dependents

Louisiana

Exemptions under the Bankruptcy Code are not available.

- Homestead: $15,000, not more than 160 acres
- Household goods: unlimited to the extent actually used by debtor or family members
- Tools of trade: to the extent necessary to exercise trade or profession
- Motor vehicle: exempt only if necessary to earn a livelihood
- Wages: 75 percent of weekly disposable wages or thirty times the weekly federal minimum hourly wage, whichever is greater
- Retirement plans: exempt, except for contributions made within one year of bankruptcy

Maine

Exemptions under the Bankruptcy Code are not available.

- Homestead: $12,500, $60,000 if debtor is disabled or more than sixty years old
- Household goods: unlimited except for any item worth more than $200
- Tools of trade: $5,000
- Motor vehicle: $2,500
- Retirement plans

Maryland

Exemptions under the Bankruptcy Code are not available.

- Homestead: $5,500 total exemptions, which may be applied to residence
- Household goods: may use general exemption of up to $500
- Tools of trade: may use general exemption of up to $2,500
- Motor vehicle: may use general exemption of up to $3,000
- Wages: 75 percent of weekly disposable wages or thirty times the weekly federal minimum hourly wage, whichever is greater
- Retirement plans

Massachusetts

Debtor can choose between state and federal exemptions.

- Homestead: $100,000
- Household goods: $3,000
- Tools of trade: $500
- Motor vehicle: $700
- Wages: amount not to exceed $125 per week
- Retirement plans

Michigan

Debtor can choose between state and federal exemptions.

- Homestead: $3,500 with a maximum forty rural acres or one lot in town
- Household goods: $1,000
- Tools of trade: $1,000
- Wages: 60 percent of the wages of a debtor with dependents, but not less than $15 per week, plus $2 per week for each person other than the debtor under eighteen years of age; if the debtor does not have a family, 40 percent of wages are exempt, but not less than $10 per week
- Retirement plans

Minnesota

Debtor can choose between state and federal exemptions.

- Homestead: unlimited in value up to 160 rural acres or one-half acre in city
- Household goods: $7,200
- Tools of trade: $8,000
- Motor vehicle: $3,200
- Wages: 75 percent of weekly disposable wages or forty times the weekly federal minimum hourly wage, whichever is greater
- Retirement plans: public employee pensions, others up to a present value of $30,000, plus additional amounts to the extent necessary for the support of debtor and dependents

Mississippi

Exemptions under the Bankruptcy Code are not available.

- Homestead: $75,000 up to 160 acres
- Personal property of any kind: may be selected up to a total value of $10,000
- Wages: 75 percent of weekly disposable wages or thirty times the weekly federal minimum hourly wage, whichever is greater
- Retirement plans

Missouri

Exemptions under the Bankruptcy Code are not available.

- Homestead: $8,000
- Household goods: $1,000
- Tools of trade: $2,000
- Motor vehicle: $1,000
- Wages: 75 percent of weekly disposable wages or thirty times the weekly federal minimum hourly wage, whichever is greater; 90 percent if debtor is head of household
- Retirement plans: public employee pensions, others to the extent necessary for support of debtor or dependents

Montana

Exemptions under the Bankruptcy Code are not available.

- Homestead: $40,000
- Household goods: $4,500, except for any item worth more than $600
- Tools of trade: $3,000
- Motor vehicle: $1,200
- Wages: 75 percent of weekly disposable wages or thirty times the weekly federal minimum hourly wage, whichever is greater
- Retirement plans

Nebraska

Exemptions under the Bankruptcy Code are not available.

- Homestead: $10,000 consisting of up to 160 rural acres or two contiguous city lots
- Household goods: $1,500
- Tools of trade: $1,500
- Miscellaneous personal property: persons who don't have a homestead may claim an additional $2,500 in any personal property, except wages
- Wages: 75 percent of weekly disposable wages or thirty times

the weekly federal minimum hourly wage, whichever is greater; 85 percent if debtor is head of household
- Retirement plans: public employee pensions, others to the extent reasonably necessary to support debtor or dependents

Nevada

Exemptions under the Bankruptcy Code are not available.

- Homestead: $125,000
- Household goods: $3,000
- Tools of trade: $4,500
- Motor vehicle: $1,500
- Wages: 75 percent of weekly disposable wages or thirty times the weekly federal minimum hourly wage, whichever is greater
- Retirement plans: public employee pensions, all others limited to $100,000

New Hampshire

Exemptions under the Bankruptcy Code are not available.

- Homestead: $30,000
- Household goods: $2,000
- Tools of trade: $1,200
- Motor vehicle: $1,000
- Wages: fifty times federal minimum wage
- Retirement plans: public employee pensions

New Jersey

Debtor can choose between state and federal exemptions.

- Household goods: $1,000
- Wages: 75 percent of weekly disposable wages or thirty times the weekly federal minimum hourly wage, whichever is greater
- Retirement plans: public employee pensions

New Mexico

Debtor can choose between state and federal exemptions.

- Homestead: $30,000
- Household goods: $500; debtors who do not own a homestead may claim an additional $2,000
- Tools of trade: $1,500
- Motor vehicle: $4,000
- Wages: 75 percent of weekly disposable wages or forty times the weekly federal minimum hourly wage, whichever is greater
- Retirement plans

New York

Exemptions under the Bankruptcy Code are not available.

- Homestead: $10,000
- Household goods: all household furniture, one refrigerator, one radio, and one TV up to a total of $5,000
- Tools of trade: $600
- Motor vehicle: $2,400
- Wages: 75 percent of weekly disposable wages or thirty times the weekly federal minimum hourly wage, whichever is greater; 90 percent for wages earned within last sixty days
- Retirement plans: public employee pensions, others to the extent needed for support

North Carolina

Exemptions under the Bankruptcy Code are not available.

- Homestead: $10,000
- Household goods: $3,500 up to as much as $6,500 when debtor has dependents
- Tools of trade: $750
- Motor vehicle: $1,500
- Wages: 75 percent of weekly disposable wages or thirty times the weekly federal minimum hourly wage, whichever is greater
- Retirement plans: public employee pensions

North Dakota

Exemptions under the Bankruptcy Code are not available.

- Homestead: $80,000 or other real or personal property in lieu of homestead of not more than $7,500
- Personal property: head of household may select personal property up to $5,000; single person may select up to $2,500
- Motor vehicle: $1,200
- Wages: 75 percent of weekly disposable wages or thirty times the weekly federal minimum hourly wage, whichever is greater
- Retirement plans: public employee pensions, all others limited to $200,000

Ohio

Exemptions under the Bankruptcy Code are not available.

- Homestead: $5,000
- Household goods: all except for any item worth more than $200
- Tools of trade: $750
- Motor vehicle: $1,000
- Wages: 75 percent of weekly disposable wages or thirty times the weekly federal minimum hourly wage, whichever is greater
- Retirement plans

Oklahoma

Exemptions under the Bankruptcy Code are not available.

- Homestead: $5,000 up to 160 acres of rural land or one acre in city
- Household goods: all
- Tools of trade: $5,000
- Motor vehicle: $3,000
- Wages: 75 percent of all earnings
- Retirement plans

Oregon

Exemptions under the Bankruptcy Code are not available.

- Homestead: $25,000, but $33,000 for joint debtors; up to 160 acres of rural land or one city block
- Household goods: $3,000
- Tools of trade: $3,000
- Motor vehicle: $1,700
- Wages: 75 percent of weekly disposable wages or $170 disposable weekly earnings, whichever is greater
- Retirement plans

Pennsylvania

Debtor can choose between state and federal exemptions.

- Personal property: wearing apparel, Bibles, schoolbooks, sewing machines, and any other personal property up to a value of $300
- Wages: all
- Retirement plans

Puerto Rico

Debtor can choose between these and federal exemptions.

- Homestead: every dwelling house on municipal lots for needy families are exempt; head of household entitled to exemption of $1,500 for other homestead property
- Household goods: $300
- Tools of trade: $300
- Motor vehicle: $500, but $6,000 if used in trade or business
- Wages: 75 percent if necessary for family use
- Retirement plans: of teachers, firefighters, and police officers

Rhode Island

Debtor can choose between state and federal exemptions.

- Household goods: $1,000
- Tools of trade: $500
- Wages: not to exceed $50
- Retirement plans

South Carolina

Debtor can choose between state and federal exemptions.

- Homestead: $5,000
- Household goods: $2,500
- Tools of trade: $750
- Motor vehicle: $1,200
- Wages: 75 percent of weekly disposable wages or thirty times the weekly federal minimum hourly wage, whichever is greater
- Retirement plans

South Dakota

Exemptions under the Bankruptcy Code are not available.

- Homestead: unlimited; if property was sold, exemption remains in proceeds for one year, up to $30,000
- Personal property: $2,000, but $4,000 for head of household
- Wages: 80 percent of disposable earnings
- Retirement plans: public employee pensions, private annuities up to $250 per month

Tennessee

Exemptions under the Bankruptcy Code are not available.

- Homestead: $5,000
- Personal property: $4,000
- Tools of trade: $750

- Wages: 75 percent of weekly disposable wages or thirty times the weekly federal minimum hourly wage, whichever is greater
- Retirement plans

Texas

Debtor can choose between state and federal exemptions.

- Homestead: unlimited in amount, up to 100 acres (200 for a head of household) in rural land or one city acre
- Personal property: up to $30,000 of selected personal property including motor vehicles, household goods, and tools of the trade; $60,000 for head of household
- Wages: 100 percent exempt
- Retirement plans

Utah

Exemptions under the Bankruptcy Code are not available.

- Homestead: $8,000, plus $2,000 for spouse and $500 for each other dependent
- Household goods: one washer and dryer, one refrigerator, one freezer, one stove, one sewing machine, all carpets, all beds and bedding
- Tools of trade: $1,500
- Wages: 75 percent of weekly disposable wages or thirty times the weekly federal minimum hourly wage, whichever is greater
- Retirement plans

Vermont

Debtor can choose between state and federal exemptions.

- Homestead: $30,000
- Household goods: $2,500
- Tools of trade: $5,000
- Motor vehicle: $2,500
- Wages: 75 percent of weekly disposable wages or thirty times the weekly federal minimum hourly wage, whichever is greater

- Retirement plans: public employee pensions, annuity contracts up to $350 per month, IRAs up to $10,000

Virgin Islands

Debtor can choose between these and federal exemptions.

- Homestead: $30,000 up to five rural acres or one-fourth acre in a city
- Household goods: $3,000
- Tools of trade: to the extent necessary for trade or occupation
- Wages: 10 percent of gross wages in excess of $30 per week
- Retirement plans: public employee pensions and annuity payments up to $250 per month

Virginia

Exemptions under the Bankruptcy Code are not available.

- Homestead: $5,000
- Household goods: $5,000
- Tools of trade: $10,000
- Motor vehicle: $2,000
- Wages: 75 percent of weekly disposable wages or thirty times the weekly federal minimum hourly wage, whichever is greater
- Retirement plans: public employee pensions, others to the extent that the debtor's interest does not provide an annual benefit in excess of $17,500

Washington

Debtor can choose between these and federal exemptions.

- Homestead: $30,000
- Household goods: $2,700
- Tools of trade: $5,000
- Motor vehicle: two vehicles up to a total value of $2,500
- Wages: 75 percent of weekly disposable wages or thirty times the weekly federal minimum hourly wage, whichever is greater
- Retirement plans

West Virginia

Exemptions under the Bankruptcy Code are not available.

- Homestead: $7,500
- Household goods: $1,000, except for any item worth more than $200
- Tools of trade: $750
- Motor vehicle: $1,200
- Wages: 80 percent of weekly disposable wages or thirty times the weekly federal minimum hourly wage, whichever is greater
- Retirement plans: public employee pensions, others to the extent necessary for support of debtor or dependents

Wisconsin

Debtor can choose between state and federal exemptions.

- Homestead: $40,000
- Household goods: $5,000
- Tools of trade: $7,500
- Motor vehicle: $1,200
- Wages: 75 percent of weekly disposable wages, limited to the extent reasonably necessary for support of debtor or dependents
- Retirement plans

Wyoming

Exemptions under the Bankruptcy Code are not available.

- Homestead: $10,000
- Household goods: $2,000
- Tools of trade: $2,000
- Motor vehicle: $2,000
- Wages: 50 percent of unearned wages to the extent necessary for support of family
- Retirement plans

Appendix 4

. . . .

YOUR MONTHLY BUDGET

A crucial step in mapping your financial future is preparation of a complete budget. This worksheet takes a lot of the pain and effort out of creating such a tool. It is divided into three sections: income, expenses, and disposable income.

INCOME

With this budget, income and expenses are figured on a monthly basis, so you may have to "pro rate" some figures. If, for example, you are paid every two weeks, you double the amount of your paycheck. If you pay car insurance every six months, divide the amount of this payment by six. If you pay some bills weekly, multiply by fifty-two and then divide by twelve to arrive at the monthly amount.

The column labeled "Mate" should be completed in all cases filed jointly by a husband and wife. Even if you are not filing a joint case, your mate's income should also be included if you are filing Chapter 13 and you live together. This is because the best-efforts test requires that all your disposable income be paid into the plan. This test takes into account the contributions others could make toward household expenses.

	DEBTOR	MATE
Current gross wages, salary, and commissions		
Estimated overtime		
1. SUBTOTAL OF WAGES & SALARY		
Payroll deductions		
Payroll taxes and social security		
Insurance		
Union dues		
Other deductions		
2. SUBTOTAL OF PAYROLL DEDUCTIONS		
TOTAL NET DEDUCTIONS		
Deduct line 2 from line 1 and enter the difference.		
Gross income from operation of business, profession, or farm (expenses of running the operation will be deducted in the "Expenses" section)		
Gross income from real property, i.e., rental income (expenses related to operation of real property will be deducted in the "Expenses" section)		
Interest and dividends		
Alimony, maintenance, or child support payments payable to you for yourself or your dependents		
List only the amount you actually receive, not the amount you're supposed to get.		
Social security or other government assistance		
Pension or retirement income		
Other income		
TOTAL INCOME		
TOTAL COMBINED INCOME Add the total monthly income of both persons and enter the sum.		

EXPENSES

Complete this section by estimating the average monthly expenses for you and your family. Do not include payments on any debt you'll be discharging in bankruptcy.

Rent or home mortgage payment	
Utilities	
Electricity and heating fuel	
Water and sewer	
Other utilities	
Home maintenance Estimate the amount you will need to spend each year for repairs and upkeep and divide that figure by twelve to arrive at a monthly amount.	
Food	
Clothing	
Laundry	
Medical expenses Include only the amount not covered by insurance. Do not include health insurance premiums in this box.	
Transportation Include gasoline and auto repairs, but don't include car payments or payments on auto insurance in this box.	
Recreation, clubs and entertainment, newspapers, magazines, etc.	
Charitable contributions	
Insurance If you pay premiums on other than a monthly basis, pro rate to determine a monthly figure. Do not list property insurance if it is included in your mortgage payment. Do not list insurance premiums that are deducted from your pay.	
Homeowner's or renter's insurance	
Life insurance	
Health insurance	
Auto insurance	

Other insurance	
Taxes Do not include taxes deducted from your pay or taxes included in your mortgage payment. If you are filing Chapter 13, don't list payments on back taxes.	
Installment payments List only the regular installment payments you'll be making despite your bankruptcy. Do not list payments on any debt you'll be discharging. Also, if filing Chapter 13, do not include payments being made through the Chapter 13 plan. In other words, if you propose to "cramdown" a loan (i.e., pay the value of the collateral through the plan), do not include any payments on that loan in this box. Or if you intend to pay a cosigned debt in full to protect your codebtor, do not include these payments here.	
Auto payments (unless the loan is being "crammed down" in Chapter 13)	
Other installment payments	
Alimony, maintenance, and child support paid to others	
Payments for support of additional dependents not living at your home	
Day care for dependents	
Total expenses from operation of business, profession, or farm	
Total expenses of operating rental income property	
TOTAL PROJECTED MONTHLY EXPENSES	

DISPOSABLE INCOME

Total combined monthly income	
Enter the total from "Income" section.	
Total projected monthly expenses	
Enter the total from "Expenses" section.	
DISPOSABLE INCOME Deduct monthly expenses from monthly income and enter the difference. If you are filing Chapter 13, also enter this amount in the "disposable income" row in the worksheet set out in appendix 5.	

Appendix 5

. . . .

CHAPTER 13 WORKSHEET

ABOUT THIS WORKSHEET

This worksheet provides an estimate of monthly payments required to fund a basic Chapter 13 plan. It addresses the typical case where the plan is funded solely by the debtor's monthly disposable income as shown in his or her budget (see appendix 4). It assumes that the amount of monthly payments will be the same. It's permissible to propose a plan that provides for higher payments in the later stages of the case, but plans constructed on the expectation of increased future income are built on a shaky foundation, and they frequently fail.

Sometimes payments into the plan are supplemented by proceeds from the sale of assets or the settling of lawsuits or by other sources of revenue. These types of plan are not common and sometimes require complex plan provisions. But even if you're contemplating this type of plan, the worksheet will still be useful because it helps you calculate the minimum amount that must be paid into the plan.

In the typical situation the *amount* of the plan payment is easy to figure. It's the same as your disposable income. The purpose of this worksheet is to figure out *the number* of payments you must make.

Remember that this worksheet produces only an estimate. Certain adjustments will have to be made to reflect the local practices of the court in your area. Also, for simplicity's sake, this worksheet does not take into account interest that in some cases must be paid on secured claims paid under the plan. Finally, bear in mind that your Chapter

13 plan payment does *not* include regular postpetition payments on your house or car. These are usually paid directly to the creditor and included as an expense under your budget.

THE SMITH'S FINANCIAL SITUATION

We've used "Joe and Mary Smith" to illustrate how to use this worksheet. The Smiths' financial affairs are probably much more complicated than yours, but if you follow along with us as we sort things out, you'll learn how to analyze your own situation.

The Smiths' home is worth $110,000. They owe $43,500 on their mortgage and are behind four payments totaling $3,200. Foreclosure proceedings have not been started. Real property taxes are not included in their mortgage payment, and they owe $1,500 to the local government.

Joe and Mary also have a rental property, a house worth $75,000, on which they still owe $70,000. Rents barely cover the mortgage payments, taxes, and upkeep, and the Smiths have always applied the income to the expenses. So the mortgage and taxes are current.

Joe owns two cars. One is a sedan worth $3,000, but he still owes $5,000, and the other is a $1,000 lemon. Mary drives a station wagon worth $4,000, which she owns free and clear.

Their paid-for household goods are worth $7,000, but the Smiths have a television and stereo they are still paying off. The TV is worth $800, and they owe $500. They owe $200 on a $500 stereo. Although their other belongings were paid off with cash, they got the cash through a $2,250 loan from a consumer finance company, which has a blanket security interest in their property.

Joe and Mary are also facing a couple of liens. There is a $10,000 judgment lien on their real property. In addition, the IRS has filed tax liens. They owe $3,000 on their 1987 income taxes, $1,200 on the 1991 taxes, and $2,750 on their 1994 taxes. But the 1994 taxes are not included in the liens.

Further, Joe is $8,500 behind in his alimony and child support.

Joe and Mary's combined disposable monthly income is $1,200. Neither has a pension. Their unsecured debts total $125,000.

In their state the Smiths are entitled to a combined homestead exemption of up to $30,000. They are each entitled to an exemption in a motor vehicle up to $1,500 and a combined exemption in household goods of up to $3,000.

Now, where do they go, and what do they consider, from here?

THE HOUSE

The amount of nonexempt equity in Joe and Mary's two parcels of real property is $40,000, before taking the IRS lien into account. If they had filed Chapter 7 instead of Chapter 13, the trustee could have sold both parcels, paid Joe and Mary the value of their homestead exemption ($30,000), and distributed the rest of the sale proceeds to creditors.

This section of the worksheet shows how Joe and Mary calculated their nonexempt equity in the real property. You can plug in your own values and see where it leads.

Note that in determining the value of real property, a good starting point is the real property tax assessment. If you purchased the home recently, the price you paid is also a good indication.

Section 1: Calculating Nonexempt Equity in Real Property

	SMITHS	YOU
1. Value of homestead property	$110,000	
2. Mortgage balances Enter the total amount due on any mortgages (not the amount you're behind, but the total amount). If the property is in foreclosure, add $1,000.	$43,500	
3. Real property taxes Enter the amount of taxes owed against the property.	$1,500	
4. Homestead exemption Enter the amount of your homestead exemption.	$30,000	
5. SUBTOTAL Add lines 2, 3, and 4 and enter the sum.	$75,000	
6. Potential nonexempt equity in homestead If line 1 is greater than line 5, enter the difference. If line 5 is greater than line 1, enter "0."	$35,000	
7. Value of nonhomestead property	$75,000	

8. Mortgage balances Enter the amount owed on all mortgages against the property.	$70,000	
9. Real property taxes Enter the amount of real property taxes owed against the property.	$0	
10. SUBTOTAL Add lines 8 and 9 and enter the sum.	$70,000	
11. Potential nonexempt equity If line 7 is greater than line 10, enter the difference. If line 10 is greater than line 7, enter "0."	$5,000	
12. Equity in all real property after deducting exemption Add lines 6 and 11 and enter the sum.	$40,000	
13. Judgment liens Enter the total amount of any judgment liens you have against you.	$10,000	
14. Secured amount of judgment Enter the lesser of line 12 or 13.	$10,000	
15. TOTAL NONEXEMPT EQUITY IN REAL PROPERTY If line 12 is greater than line 14, enter the difference. If line 14 is greater than line 12, enter "0."	$30,000	

THE CARS

Since Joe still owes $5,000 on a sedan worth only $3,000, there's no equity in the vehicle. The Smiths will use their "cramdown" powers to pay off that car by paying what it's worth (as opposed to how much is owed).

Meanwhile, Joe's other car is worth $1,000, which is less than the $1,500 he is allowed under the exemption. But Mary's station wagon is worth $4,000, which exceeds the allowable exemption by $2,500. If they had filed Chapter 7, the trustee could have sold this car, paid Mary her $1,500 exemption, and distributed the rest to creditors.

In adapting this section of the worksheet to your own situation, keep in mind that in most states debtors are entitled to exempt one car (or one car each in a jointly filed bankruptcy case). So if you own more than one vehicle, you have to choose which one to use the exemption on. Of course, if you owe more than a car is worth—as is Joe's situation with the sedan—there is no equity, so it doesn't figure in the calculations below.

Courts disagree on how cars should be valued, but a good estimate would be the average between the "high" and "low" values stated in the Kelly Blue Book.

Section 2: Calculating Nonexempt Equity in Motor Vehicles

	SMITHS	YOU
1. Net value of any vehicles not claimed as exempt	$0	
2. Net value of vehicle claimed as exempt	$1,000	
3. Exemption Enter the amount of the allowable exemption.	$1,500	
4. Nonexempt value of vehicle If line 2 is greater than line 3, enter the difference. If line 3 is greater than line 2, enter "0."	$0	
5. Net value of second vehicle claimed as exempt Enter the net value of a second vehicle only if this is a joint case.	$4,000	
6. Exemption Enter the amount of the allowable exemption in the second car.	$1,500	
7. Nonexempt value of second vehicle If line 5 is greater than line 6, enter the difference. If line 6 is greater than line 5, enter "0."	$2,500	
8. TOTAL NONEXEMPT EQUITY IN VEHICLES Add lines 1, 4, and 7 and enter the sum.	$2,500	

HOUSEHOLD GOODS AND OTHER ASSETS

Joe and Mary have paid for all of their remaining assets except for the television and stereo. They have equity of $300 in the television because it's worth $800 and they owe $500 and equity of $300 in the stereo, which is worth $500 and for which they owe $200.

If either the television or stereo was worth less than was owed against them, the plan would propose to pay only the value of the item (as in the case of Joe's sedan). Here, since the Smiths are current on their loans, they will continue to make regular payments directly to the creditor.

However, there is also the $2,250 they owe on a finance company loan, which was hedged on a blanket security interest. Since the value of the Smiths' household goods exceeds $3,000, they can't eliminate the lien (see chapter 7, "Games People Play").

This section of the worksheet is designed to help you determine the nonexempt value of assets other than real property or cars.

Several observations before you get started:

• The value of all assets not subject to a purchase money security interest should be totaled and entered on line 1.

• Line 2 is used for all items that are subject to a purchase money security interest. It is the total net value of all assets subject to purchase money security interests.

• Net value of an asset refers to its value after deducting any purchase money security interest that is attached to it. For example, if your TV is worth $800 and you still owe $500, the net value is $300.

• Any equity you might have in any of your household goods is further reduced by the amount of any nonpurchase money blanket security interest that you may have given to secure a loan.

Section 3: Calculating Nonexempt Value of Assets Other Than Real Property or Cars

	SMITHS	YOU
1. Total value of all household goods and other assets owned free and clear Add the value of all these items and enter the sum.	$7,000	
2. Net value of any household goods and other assets that are subject to a purchase money security interest Where any asset is subject to a purchase money security interest, deduct the amount owed against that asset from its value to arrive at the net value. Add the net values of any household goods and other assets that are subject to purchase money security interests and enter the total.	$600	
3. SUBTOTAL Add lines 1 and 2 and enter the sum.	$7,600	

4. Amount of allowable exemption Enter the maximum amount of the exemption allowed in your state (see appendix 3, "Exemption Laws").	$3,000	
5. Potential exempt amount If line 3 is greater than line 4, enter the difference. If line 4 is greater than line 3, enter "0."	$4,600	
6. Amount owed on nonpurchase money security interests Enter the total amount owed.	$2,250	
7. Secured amount of nonpurchase money security interests Enter the lesser of line 6 or 5.	$2,250	
8. Nonexempt amount If line 5 is greater than line 7, enter the difference. If line 7 is greater than line 5, enter "0."	$2,350	

TAXES

oe and Mary owe federal income taxes for three years: $3,000 for 1987, $1,200 for 1991, and $2,750 for 1994. In the Notice of Tax Lien (see the discussion of tax liens in chapter 4 and the section on dealing with the IRS in chapter 13), the IRS mentions the 1987 debt, even though it is old enough to be dischargeable, and the 1991 bill. The 1994 taxes are not specified in the notice, but they are not dischargeable.

Determining the impact of nonproperty taxes in a Chapter 13 bankruptcy can be difficult and confusing. This section of the worksheet separates taxes into dischargeable and nondischargeable taxes (refer to the discussion of dischargeable taxes in chapter 4; see also appendix 2, table 4 for help in determining which taxes are dischargeable). The section also distinguishes between those taxes covered by a tax lien and those that are not.

All of this is confusing because these figures overlap. Taxes covered by a tax lien can be nondischargeable, dischargeable—or both. And nondischargeable taxes can include some that are covered by a tax lien and some that are not. The information that follows will help you sort this out.

Section 4: Calculating Nonproperty Tax Liability

	SMITHS	YOU
1. Dischargeable taxes mentioned in tax lien	$3,000	
2. Nondischargeable taxes mentioned in tax lien	$1,200	
3. Total taxes mentioned in tax liens Add lines 1 and 2 and enter the sum.	$4,200	
4. Nondischargeable taxes not mentioned in tax lien	$2,750	
5. Total nondischargeable taxes Add lines 2 and 4 and enter the sum.	$3,950	
6. Total nondischargeable taxes and dischargeable taxes claimed under tax lien(s) Add lines 1 and 5 and enter the sum.	$6,950	

STRAIGHT BANKRUPTCY AND
UNSECURED CREDITORS

This section of the worksheet shows how much money would be paid to unsecured priority and nonpriority (general) creditors if the Smiths had filed Chapter 7 instead of Chapter 13. The reason this is relevant is because of the best-interest test, which requires that general unsecured creditors in Chapter 13 receive at least as much as they would have received if the case were filed under Chapter 7, instead of Chapter 13.

Section 5: Calculating Amount Owed to
Unsecured Creditors in a Chapter 7

	SMITHS	YOU
1. Real property Enter the total from section 1, line 15.	$30,000	
2. Motor vehicles Enter the total from section 2, line 8.	$2,500	
3. Household goods and other assets Enter the total from section 3, line 8.	$2,350	

4. SUBTOTAL Add lines 1, 2, and 3 and enter the sum.	$34,850	
5. Tax liens Enter the lesser of line 4 above or line 3 of section 4.	$4,200	
6. TOTAL AMOUNT THAT UNSECURED CREDITORS WOULD HAVE RECEIVED IN CHAPTER 7 If line 4 is greater than line 5, enter the difference. If line 5 is greater than line 4, enter "0."	$30,650	

STRAIGHT BANKRUPTCY AND PRIORITY CLAIMS

In the preceding section, we calculated how much money all unsecured creditors would receive if Joe and Mary had filed Chapter 7. Here we examine unsecured, nondischargeable taxes. Such taxes, as well as alimony and child support (see section 7 below), are all priority claims, which means they are paid in full before other unsecured creditors are paid anything.

Priority claims have to be calculated and deducted from the amount available to all unsecured creditors to determine how much nonpriority creditors would receive in a Chapter 7. This is the amount that must be paid to satisfy the best-interest test (see section 11 below).

As you work through this, be aware that if line 3 of section 4 (the total amount of taxes mentioned in tax liens) is greater than line 5 of section 5 (the value of assets possibly subject to tax liens), then the value of the property securing tax liens is not enough to secure both dischargeable and nondischargeable taxes. In this situation the value of the property will be assigned to dischargeable taxes first.

Section 6: Calculating Unsecured, Nondischargeable Taxes

	SMITHS	YOU
1. Value of property subject to tax liens Enter the amount from section 5, line 5.	$4,200	
2. Dischargeable taxes mentioned in tax lien Enter the amount from section 4, line 1.	$3,000	

3. Secured dischargeable taxes Enter the lesser of line 1 or 2.	$3,000	
4. Value remaining after satisfaction of dischargeable taxes If line 1 is greater than line 2, enter the difference. If line 2 is greater than line 1, enter "0."	$1,200	
5. Total nondischargeable taxes Enter the amount from section 4, line 5.	$3,950	
6. Secured nondischargeable taxes If line 5 is "0," enter "0" in this line also; otherwise, enter the lesser of line 4 above or line 2 of section 4. If they are the same, enter this amount.	$1,200	
7. Unsecured, nondischargeable taxes Deduct line 6 from line 5 and enter the difference.	$2,750	

Section 7: Calculating Total Priority Claims

	SMITHS	YOU
1. Alimony and child support Enter the amount of back child support and alimony you owe. Do not include divorce obligations that are property settlements rather than alimony. Enter only the amount you are behind (payments accruing postpetition will be paid outside the plan and included as an expense in your budget).	$8,500	
2. Unsecured, nondischargeable taxes Enter the amount from section 6, line 7.	$2,750	
3. Total priority claims Add lines 1 and 2 and enter the sum.	$11,250	

DISPOSABLE INCOME

After completing their monthly budget, Joe and Mary calculated that once all current expenses are paid, they should have $1,200 left over.

Disposable income is the amount you have left over each month, after paying all your current bills. If you haven't already done so, you can calculate your own disposable income using the budget worksheet in appendix 4.

Note that your monthly disposable income is equivalent to the amount of your plan payment.

Section 8: Amount of Monthly Disposable Income

	SMITHS	YOU
Amount of monthly disposable income	$1,200	

RETAINING PROPERTY

Joe and Mary intend to make up back payments on their home mortgage, continue paying for their TV and stereo, and, as to the remaining secured claims, pay the value of the collateral securing the debts. Reason: they want to keep the items they've got.

There are various ways and means to keep property that secures a loan.

If you want to keep your home, back payments would be paid through the plan and payments falling due postpetition would be paid directly to the creditor. For a car or other personal property, you could pay the value of the item through the plan. Or you could treat it the same as your house (that is, "cure" back payments through the plan and make postpetition payments directly to the creditor).

If, on the other hand, you intend to allow foreclosure of your real property, don't enter any amount in the "mortgage arrearages," "real property taxes," or "judgment liens" lines below. Similarly, if you intend to surrender your car or other collateral, don't enter any amount in those lines.

Tax liens are stickier because they attach to essentially all your earthly belongings. Your plan may propose to surrender all your assets to the taxing authority in full satisfaction of a tax lien. (As a practical matter, unless you own land, have a pension, or other liquid assets, the taxing authority won't bother taking your stuff.) But this strategy doesn't help if you have nondischargeable taxes, since they will have to be paid whether there is a tax lien or not.

Section 9: Calculating Total Secured Claims

	SMITHS	YOU
1. Mortgage arrearages Enter the amount you are behind on any mortgages. Add $1,000 if foreclosure proceedings have been started. Do not include the monthly payments falling due after the petition date because these payments are usually made directly to the creditor and are already included in your budget.	$3,200	
2. Real property taxes Enter the amount of past-due real property taxes, unless they are included in your monthly mortgage payment and are included in the arrearage entered above.	$1,500	
3. If your car is worth less than is owed on it . . . Enter the value of the car. Since you will be paying the full value of the car through the plan, you won't be making any of the regular payments.	$3,000	
4. If your car is worth more than you owe on it . . . Enter the amount you are behind in payments. Back payments are included in your plan; postpetition payments are usually paid directly to the creditor.	$0	
5. Purchase money security interests in assets worth less than the debt Enter the value of the assets. This is like paying the value of collateral instead of the amount owed.	$0	
6. Purchase money security interests in assets worth more than the debt Enter the amount you are behind. Postpetition payments will be paid directly to the creditor.	$0	
7. Secured amount of nonpurchase money security interests Enter the amount from section 3, line 7.	$2,250	
8. Secured taxes Enter the amount from section 5, line 5.	$4,200	
9. Secured judgments Enter the amount from section 1, line 14.	$10,000	
10. Total secured claims to be paid under the plan Add lines 1–9 above and enter the sum.	$24,150	

COSIGNED LOANS

oe and Mary don't have any cosigned debts, but if you do, fill in the line below.

One of the unique benefits of Chapter 13 is the *codebtor stay*. If your plan proposes to pay a cosigned loan in full, the creditor cannot collect from your cosigner. But this is up to you. You don't have to provide for payment of cosigned loans. But if you don't, the creditor can go after the cosigner.

Section 10: Amount of Cosigned Loan(s)

	SMITHS	YOU
If you want to prevent a creditor on a cosigned loan(s) from going after your cosigner . . . Enter the full amount of the cosigned loan(s).	$0	

BEST-INTEREST REQUIREMENT

s noted earlier, the best-interest test requires that general, unsecured creditors in Chapter 13 be paid at least as much as they would receive if your case had been filed under Chapter 7. This means that you must pay the value of any nonexempt equity into the plan for the benefit of unsecured creditors—unless, of course, your plan proposes to pay them 100 percent.

But watch for this twist: in a Chapter 7 unsecured creditors receive only what's left over after priority claims are paid in full. In a Chapter 13 you can "apply" the best-interest portion of your Chapter 13 payment to any priority (and also nondischargeable) claims such as taxes, alimony, and child support.

If you have a $5,000 boat and owe $3,000 in alimony, you still have to pay the value of the boat into the plan, but $3,000 will be applied to satisfy your alimony obligation. In other words, the money that would otherwise have gone to general unsecured creditors goes to priority claims that you would have had to pay anyway. It's a good deal for you, but not for your general, unsecured creditors.

Section 11: Calculating Amount of Best-Interest Requirement

	SMITHS	YOU
1. Equity in nonexempt assets Enter the amount from section 5, line 6.	$30,650	
2. Priority claims Enter the amount from section 7, line 3.	$11,250	
3. Total needed to satisfy the best-interest requirement If line 1 is greater than line 2, enter the difference. If line 2 is greater than line 1, enter "0."	$19,400	

ATTORNEY FEES

In Chapter 13 the amount of attorney fees usually depends on how much work your case requires. A portion is paid before filing, and the balance is included in your plan payment. One thousand dollars is probably a safe estimate of the attorney fees to be paid through the plan.

Section 12: Estimate of Attorney Fees

	SMITHS	YOU
Estimate of total attorney fees	$1,000	

TRUSTEE'S COMMISSION

The Chapter 13 trustee is entitled to a commission, ranging from 7 to 10 percent of the payments you make into the plan. The commission is based on payments on mortgage and car arrearages, "cramdown" payments, payments on priority claims, any best-interest payments, and attorney fees paid through the plan. House and car payments falling due after the petition date frequently (depending on local practice) can be paid outside the plan (that is, directly to the creditor) and are not subject to the trustee's commission.

Section 13: Calculating Trustee's Commission

	SMITHS	YOU
1. Total claims to be paid through the plan Add the totals shown in sections 7, 9, 10, 11, and 12 and enter the sum.	$55,800	
2. Trustee's commission Multiply the amount in line 1 by 10 percent and enter the product.	$5,580	

AMOUNT NEEDED TO FUND YOUR PLAN

This section of the worksheet establishes the minimum amount required to fund your Chapter 13 plan.

Since we've assumed that you expect your disposable income to remain about the same, the number of payments you have to make is simply the amount required to fund the plan divided by the amount of your disposable income.

There are a couple of wrinkles, however. The best-efforts test requires that you contribute your disposable income into the plan for at least thirty-six months or until all your debts are paid in full, whichever occurs first. It's rare that Chapter 13 debtors are able to pay all their debts in full within thirty-six months, so in most cases the best-efforts test requires at least thirty-six payments.

Section 14: Calculating Minimum Amount Needed for Plan and Number of Payments

	SMITHS	YOU
1. Total unsecured debts Total all unsecured debts, including the unsecured portion of partially secured debts, plus unsecured tax debts.	$125,000	
2. Disposable income for next three years Multiply your monthly disposable income (section 8) by thirty-six and enter the product.	$43,200	

3. Best-efforts test Enter the lesser of line 1 or 2. The best-efforts test requires that at least this much be paid into any Chapter 13 plan unless unsecured creditors are paid in full.	$43,200	
4. Amount needed to pay secured and priority claims, and also satisfy the best-interest test Add lines 1 and 2 from section 13 and enter the sum.	$61,380	
5. Minimum amount needed to fund plan Enter the greater of line 3 or 4.	$61,380	
6. Number of payments required to complete plan Divide the amount in line 3 above by the amount of your disposable income from section 8 and enter the quotient. If the number of payments is greater than sixty, your plan is not feasible. You'll have to consider surrendering some collateral or not paying cosigned debts. Any number less than sixty will be feasible, but the closer you come to this sixty-month limit, the more difficult your plan will be to complete. Usually, if you miss plan payments for a good reason, your plan can just be extended to make up these payments. But if the plan is already sixty months, it can't be extended.	51.15	

SUMMARY

The Smiths' monthly payment is the amount of their disposable income: $1,200. They'll have to make full payments for fifty-one months and a partial payment to complete their plan. The maximum length of any Chapter 13 plan is sixty months, so Joe and Mary will have to be diligent in making their payments. Even if they have a good reason, they will not be allowed to miss more than seven payments.

Section 15: Summary of Plan

	SMITHS	YOU
1. Amount of your monthly plan payment Enter the amount of disposable income from section 8.	$1,200	
2. Number of payments that will be required Enter the amount from section 14, line 6.	51.5	

GLOSSARY

Automatic Stay: A court order that goes into effect automatically the moment a bankruptcy petition is filed. It stops creditors from garnishing wages, initiating lawsuits, repossessing property, or even contacting debtors.

Avoidance Powers: As an adversarial process, the law provides debtors, creditors, and trustees with certain legal weapons and expects them to duke it out. Avoidance powers give trustees and debtors the right to cancel certain types of liens and transfers.

Bankruptcy: A legal process through which people can obtain a "fresh start" in their financial life. That fresh start is achieved through the elimination of all or a portion of debts or by structuring payments over a three- to five-year period.

Bankruptcy Court: A federal court established by Congress to hear bankruptcy cases and related proceedings. Appeals from this court are heard by either a bankruptcy appellate panel or a federal district court. Further appeal is to one of the eleven U.S. courts of appeal and then to the Supreme Court.

Bankruptcy Judge: A jurist, appointed by a circuit court, who presides over federal bankruptcy matters.

Bankruptcy Reform Act of 1994: A series of amendments to the U.S. Bankruptcy Code that went into effect in October 1994. The legislation has an enormous impact on consumer debtors because it changes the game rules for alimony and child support, increases the debt limits for some filers, prohibits discrimination against student loan applicants, doubles the amount of property debtors get to keep, and modifies many other bankruptcy issues.

Best-Efforts Test: One of the two tests (see *best-interest test*) that must be met in a Chapter 13 filing. Essentially, it holds that you must make your "best effort" to repay your debts by putting all disposable income into the plan for at least three years.

Best-Interest Test: One of the two tests (see *best-efforts test*) that must be met in a Chapter 13 filing. Essentially, it holds that unsecured creditors must be paid at least as much as they would have received if the case had been filed under Chapter 7.

Bifurcation: Legalese for "split into two parts." It comes into play only in Chapter 13 bankruptcy cases and means that a secured claim can be divided. This tactic can be a tremendous benefit for the debtor. In some cases it can be used to reduce home mortgage debts.

Chapter 7: Often referred to as *straight bankruptcy* and frequently what people think of when they hear the term *bankruptcy*. Chapter 7 is a section of the U.S. Bankruptcy Code under which a person's property can be sold and the proceeds split among creditors.

Chapter 11: The chapter of the U.S. Bankruptcy Code that allows businesses to restructure under the direction of the court.

Chapter 12: The chapter of the U.S. Bankruptcy Code reserved for family farmers.

Chapter 13: Often referred to as *wage earner's bankruptcy*. Chapter 13 is a section of the U.S. Bankruptcy Code that permits a person to retain assets and pay off debts, in whole or part, over a three- to five-year period.

Chapter "20": There is no Chapter 20 in the Bankruptcy Code. The phrase is slang referring to the strategy of filing a Chapter 13 immediately after a Chapter 7 (7 + 13 = 20) to accomplish things that aren't possible under either chapter alone.

Collateral Estoppel: A legal doctrine that prevents retrying in one court an issue that was already litigated in another court. If, prepetition, a creditor wins a lawsuit against you claiming you are guilty of fraud or other misconduct, you may not be allowed to dispute these allegations when you file bankruptcy.

Collection Information Statement (CIS): An extensive financial disclosure statement that must be submitted to the IRS in support of an Offer in Compromise or request for an Installment Payment Plan. It shows the IRS your financial condition but also tells it where all your assets are located.

Community Property States: In nine states (Arizona, California, Idaho, Louisiana, Nevada, New Mexico, Texas, Washington, and Wisconsin), the earnings of either spouse are deemed the property of both, and any property obtained during the marriage—with the usual exception of inheritances—is considered the property of both the husband and wife.

Confirmation: A court order making a Chapter 13 plan binding on the debtor and all creditors. If the trustee or a creditor objects to a proposed plan, a court hearing is required, but in most cases plans are approved as a matter of course.

Consumer Credit Counsel Service (CCCS): A nonprofit group created and maintained by large institutional creditors that helps people set up debt repayment plans.

Contempt: An act of disrespect toward the court, such as deliberate disobedience of a court order or conduct that tends to obstruct the court's function. Contempt can result in a fine or imprisonment.

Court Filing Fee: The amount of money you must pay to file a legal action, such as a bankruptcy petition. For a bankruptcy case, the fee is $175.

Cramdown: Refers to a restructuring of loans in a Chapter 13 without the consent of the creditor. For instance, if you owe $10,000 on your car, but it's worth only $8,000, the court will approve a "cramdown" of the loan to an $8,000 secured claim.

Cure: The legal term for the correction of a deficiency or defect. In a Chapter 13 case it refers to the process of making up back mortgage payments.

Debt Collectors: People hired to recover debts. Although they would love for you to think otherwise, debt collectors have virtually no power. They are not allowed to threaten or harass you. They generally cannot contact you at odd hours or at work. If you tell them to leave you alone, they must.

Debtor: A person who owes money to another person. In the context of a bankruptcy case, the debtor is the person who files bankruptcy.

Debtors' Exam: A state court proceeding where the debtors are hauled into court to answer questions about assets and debts.

Default Judgment: A judgment entered against a person without a trial. Most commonly occurs when someone fails to file opposing papers within thirty days after being served with a summons and complaint in a lawsuit.

Denial of Discharge: When the court refuses to erase any debts. This can occur if the debtor conceals assets, disobeys an order of the court, or commits fraud. If discharge is denied, the debtor will have surrendered all nonexempt property, will still be responsible for the debts, and will still have a bankruptcy listed on his or her credit record.

Discharge: The term used to describe what happens to debts when they are eliminated by the court.

Dismissal: Ending a bankruptcy before it's complete. Once a bankruptcy is dismissed, creditors are free to resume collection efforts. Chapter 13 cases can be voluntarily ended by the debtor or the trustee. Or a creditor can ask the court to terminate the case because the debtor is not living up to his or her obligations under the U.S. Bankruptcy Code. Chapter 7 cases are rarely dismissed, and, unlike with a Chapter 13, a debtor cannot end a Chapter 7 without the trustee's and creditor's consent.

Dragnet Clause: A contractual stipulation that allows a lender to, in effect, turn an unsecured debt into a secured one. Often, when a borrower has two loans with the same finance company, such as one for cash and another for a car, a clause in the contract allows the lender to commingle the terms. This means that even when the cash loan is unsecured and separate from the car loan, if the funds were borrowed from the same finance company, the car could be in jeopardy if the cash loan isn't paid.

Drop-Dead Agreement: A common type of settlement agreement by a secured creditor in Chapter 13, where the creditor agrees to withdraw its motion for relief from stay, in exchange for the debtor's agreement that if any additional payments are missed, the creditor may simply present an order to the bankruptcy court allowing foreclosure.

Due-on-Sale Clause: A provision lurking in the fine print of many mortgages that says, essentially, that if the property is sold or becomes the target of a lien, the entire loan becomes due immediately.

Dummy Return: A tax return that a taxing entity—such as the IRS—files for you if you fail to file.

Employee Retirement Income Security Act of 1974 (ERISA): A federal law enacted to protect pension rights of nongovernment employees. If a pension meets ERISA requirements, it is protected in bankruptcy.

Equal Credit Opportunity Act (ECOA): A federal law forbidding lenders from discrimination on the basis of gender, marital status, race, religion, or age.

Equity: A person's interest in property after subtracting what is owed. For instance, if you have a house worth $100,000 and you owe the bank $80,000, your equity is $20,000.

Exempt Property: Property that is protected, under state or federal law, from the claims of creditors. Different states have different exemptions, but most exempt homesteads, pensions, wages, one car, and household goods.

Fair Credit Reporting Act: A federal law giving consumers the right to dispute or correct their credit reports.

Fair Debt Collection Practices Act: A consumer protection act designed to eliminate improper and inappropriate debt collection tactics, such as calling the debtor at work or at unreasonable hours, making unwarranted threats, or using foul or abusive language.

Family Farmer: In the case of an individual, a farmer whose debts do not exceed $1.5 million, 80 percent of which arise from farming, and who in the past year received more than 50 percent of his or her income from farming.

Foreclosure: The way a lien creditor collects on its lien, usually by a forced sale of the collateral. When the collateral is real property, an actual lawsuit is frequently, but not always, required. Many states provide a method of nonjudicial foreclosure where the collateral is sold at public auction after a specified period of time after notice of the sale is given. Typically the time period is about four months. When the collateral is personal property, a nonjudicial sale can be held with as little as ten days' notice. Foreclosure should be distinguished from repossession, which, by itself, doesn't terminate the debtor's interest in the collateral.

Fraudulent Transfer: A transfer of property made with the intention of shielding it from creditors.

Fresh Start: A crucial principle to the American concept of bankruptcy. Under U.S. laws, debts can be forgiven and the debtor provided with a new financial life.

Garnishment: The legal phrase for a situation in which a creditor collects a debt from a third person. For example, if you owe somebody money, he or she can require your employer to withhold a portion of your wages.

Hardship Discharge: A Chapter 13 discharge that may be available even though the debtor is unable to complete plan payments. The court must conclude that the debtor did his or her best, and that creditors received at least as much as they would have if the case had been filed under Chapter 7.

Health Education Assistance Loans (HEAL): Student loans for medical school. Ordinary student loans are discharged in bankruptcy if repayment would impose an "undue hardship." HEAL loans are not dischargeable unless requiring repayment would be "unconscionable."

Homestead Exemption: A legal perk that protects your homestead from creditors. Almost every state offers this exemption to bankruptcy, shielding some or all of the equity in a debtor's home.

Insiders: Relatives and others who have a strong influence on the debtor. Prepetition payments that are made within a year of the petition date and that benefit insiders may sometimes be recovered by the trustee.

Joint Bankruptcy: A bankruptcy petition filed by a husband and wife.

Lien: A legal right or interest in another's property that remains in effect until a debt is paid. For instance, someone with a lien on your car would have rights to the value of your vehicle, to the extent of the debt. A lien holder could force the sale of the car to recover whatever she or he is owed.

National Health Services Corporation (NHSC) Scholarships: Scholarships offered by the National Health Service Corporation to medical students. In exchange for such a scholarship, the student promises that upon graduation, he or she will practice in a medically neglected area of the country one year for each year of benefits received. If the promise is broken, the doctor has to pay damages equal to three times the amount of the scholarship, frequently hundreds of thousands of dollars. This obligation cannot be discharged in bankruptcy unless requiring repayment would be "unconscionable."

No-Asset Case: A Chapter 7 case in which there are no assets available for the creditors to take.

Notice of Tax Lien: A filing by the IRS in the public records giving it an enforceable lien on all earthly belongings of a taxpayer. If the notice is filed before a bankruptcy petition, taxes can be much more difficult to discharge.

Offer in Compromise: A formal offer to the IRS that, if accepted and performed, satisfies a tax obligation for less than the amount owed.

180-Day Rule: A general rule that under certain circumstances prohibits the filing of a bankruptcy petition within 180 days of the date when a previous petition was dismissed.

Perfection of Lien: The act of making a lien enforceable by recording it in the public records or having it noted on the certificate of title to a motor vehicle.

Personal Property: Everything that is not land or permanently attached to land. Some states treat mobile homes as personal property, whereas others treat them as land.

Petition Date: The date when a bankruptcy petition is filed. The precise date is important in determining exactly when bankruptcy takes effect, which debts are eliminated, and what property is affected.

Preferential Transfer: A transfer of property, sometimes on the eve of bankruptcy, that gives a creditor an unfair advantage. For example, if the month before bankruptcy you repaid $1,500 on a past-due debt—and thereby reduced the pot of assets available to other creditors—the payment could be considered a preferential transfer and could be voided.

Priority Claims: Claims that the trustee pays ahead of other claims. The most common are taxes, child support, and alimony. In a Chapter 13 the plan must propose to pay these claims in full. In a Chapter 7 asset case the debtor should make sure that a proof of claim is filed for these claims because any unpaid balance will not be discharged.

Proof of Claim: A document a creditor must file with the court if he or she hopes to receive at least partial payment from a bankrupt debtor. Creditors usually have ninety days after the 341 meeting to file proof that they are owed money. In some situations a debtor might want to file a proof of claim on behalf of a creditor to make sure a particular debt is paid by the trustee.

Property of the Estate: Simply, the property that is subject to the bankruptcy process. It includes all property rights owned as of the petition date, plus inheritances, life insurance benefits, and divorce settlements received within 180 days thereafter. In a Chapter 13 it also includes postpetition wages earned during the case.

Purchase Money Security Interest: A security interest voluntarily given in personal property to secure payment of its purchase price. It can be created in favor of the seller of the item or a lender who provides the funds for the purchase of a specific item. A purchase money security interest can be converted to nonpurchase money status because of a refinancing or if subsequent purchases are added as security for the loan.

Reaffirmation: A procedure in which a Chapter 7 debtor can "reaffirm" or take responsibility for all or part of a debt, despite bankruptcy. People usually reaffirm in order to keep property on which a creditor has a lien. Sometimes debtors reaffirm in order to preserve credit privileges with a particular creditor or to settle a dischargeability claim.

Real Property: Land and things permanently attached to land, such as buildings, fences, built-in swimming pools. States disagree on whether mobile homes are real property or personal property.

Redemption: Literally, it means "to pay buy back." In a Chapter 7 bankruptcy it refers to the practice of releasing property from a security interest by paying only the value of the collateral, instead of the whole debt. Outside of bankruptcy it describes the right of a property owner to get his or her property back after a foreclosure sale by paying the whole amount of the debt.

Relief from Stay: When a creditor gets permission to proceed against the debtor or the debtor's property despite the automatic stay. Usually, creditors want to repossess or foreclose on collateral. In a Chapter 7 case a creditor must show that the debtor is in default on the debt and that the property is not worth more than the debt. In a Chapter 13 case a creditor must also show that the property is not necessary for the debtor's financial reorganization (the debtor's home is almost always necessary) or that the debtor failed to make postpetition payments.

Repossession: Where a creditor obtains possession of collateral after default. Compare *foreclosure,* which actually terminates the debtor's interest in the collateral. Repossession most often involves personal property, and a creditor's rights are quite limited. Unless the creditor gets a court order (which rarely happens), it cannot "breach the peace" to repossess collateral. Courts differ on what constitutes a "breach of the peace," but a creditor certainly cannot enter a debtor's home to seize possessions and cannot break into a locked garage to repossess a car. A creditor can, however, repossess a car from a public street and probably from a private driveway. And there is no requirement that the creditor give advance notice of its plan to repossess.

Restitution: A court order, imposed as a result of a criminal conviction, requiring the defendant to pay money, either to the victim or to a government agency, to compensate for the damages caused to the victim. In some cases failure to make restitution payments can land a person in jail.

Secured Debt: A debt that is backed up by collateral. For example, when you purchase an item at some department stores, the item serves as collateral for the debt. That means if you can't make the payments, the store can take back the VCR, refrigerator, or whatever it was that you bought.

Security Interest: A lien on personal property that you agree to give a creditor.

Spendthrift Trust: This type of trust is established for the benefit of another person and provides that the trust property cannot be seized by the beneficiary's creditors.

Statute of Limitations: A law that sets the time period during which a lawsuit or legal action must be initiated. Usually, the statute of limitations is six years on a debt. In other words, if the creditor waits longer than six years, it's probably too late. However, if a judgment has been entered, the collection period can span twenty years.

Substantial Abuse: The rare situation where a debtor doesn't really need a Chapter 7 discharge because he or she had enough disposable income to pay all the debts within three years. The court will then dismiss a bankruptcy unless the debtor converts the case to Chapter 13.

Taxpayer Assistance Order: An order issued by the taxpayer ombudsman suspending arbitrary collection or other activities of the IRS that are causing a taxpayer "significant hardship."

Tenancy by the Entirety: An ancient concept, still embraced by some states, where creditors of one spouse may not seize property owned jointly by both spouses.

341 Meeting: Named for a section of the Bankruptcy Code, this session is a meeting attended by the debtor, the debtor's attorney, a trustee, and any creditors who choose to appear.

Trust Fund Taxes: Taxes that an employer is supposed to withhold from an employee's pay and turn over to the government, including the employee's share of social security (FICA). An employer who files bankruptcy can't discharge these taxes unless they are more than ten years old. If the employer is a corporation, these taxes can be collected from the corporate officer or employee who is responsible for withholding them.

Trustee: A private person appointed to represent the interests of creditors in bankruptcy. His or her job is to obtain as much of the debtor's property as possible to satisfy creditors' claims. In compensation, the trustee gets a cut of whatever is recovered.

Truth in Lending Act (TILA): A law that requires home mortgage lenders to provide written notification of all charges connected to your loan, and in some cases to notify you that you have a right to cancel the transaction. In a bankruptcy case TILA may allow a debtor to remove a lien without paying the debt.

U.S. Bankruptcy Code: A comprehensive law enacted by Congress pursuant to an express provision of the U.S. Constitution, which takes precedence over any inconsistent state laws.

Unsecured Debt: The opposite of a secured debt, an unsecured debt is not backed up by collateral. Although someone with an unsecured debt can sue you, he or she cannot take your personal property.

INDEX